Sonny Sez!

Sonny Sez!

Legends, Yarns & Downright Truths

SONNY ELIOT

DRAWINGS BY DRAPER HILL

Edited by Stanley D. Williams

Foreword by Dick Guindon

A Painted Turtle book
Detroit, Michigan

Library of Congress Cataloging-in-Publication Data

Eliot, Sonny, 1922–
Sonny sez! : legends, yarns, and downright truths /
text by Sonny Eliot ; drawings by Draper Hill ;
edited by Stanley D. Williams.
p. cm. – (A painted turtle book)
ISBN-13: 978-0-8143-3335-8 (pbk. : alk. paper)
ISBN-10: 0-8143-3335-4 (pbk. : alk. paper)
1. Curiosities and wonders. 2. Handbooks, vade-mecums, etc.
I. Hill, Draper. II. Williams, Stanley D., 1947– III. Title.
AG106.E45 2007
031.02—dc22
2007010245

∞ The paper used in this publication meets the minimum requirements
of the American National Standard for Information Sciences—
Permanence of Paper for Printed Library Materials, ANSI Z39.48-
1984.

Grateful acknowledgment is made to the Leonard and Harriette
Simons Endowed Family Fund for generous support of the publication
of this volume.

Published with the assistance of a fund established by Thelma Gray
James of Wayne State University for the publication of folklore and
English studies.

Designed and typeset by Maya Rhodes
Composed in News Gothic and HandPrinting
Drawing cleanup by Robert and David Thrasher

Contents

= story included on audio CD

Contents

Contents

Foreword

Here is knowledge, and since knowledge is power, think of this book as a weapon and don't point it at anybody. Inside you'll find a lifetime of wisdom gleaned by Sonny Eliot's love of language. We think that this love came about because of an impoverished childhood. Growing up without toys, Sonny was forced to play with words. BA-BOOM! This book is evidence that he's not lost that love or his childhood. Draper Hill is just as bad and appears here as his enabler.

DICK GUINDON

A young Sonny Eliot at play.

Acknowledgments

This book would not be, except for the gracious enthusiasm shown to us by Jane Hoehner and the many individuals of stupendous talent at Wayne State University Press who have helped us along the way, especially Maya Rhodes, Carrie Downes Teefey, and Jennifer Backer. Thank you for removing the rocks along the path—sorry we put them there in the first place, but we were just trying to help.

And we would be terribly remiss—and a mess too, we might add—if we didn't thank our beautiful, charming, and resplendent wives, Annette, Sarah, and Pam, for putting up with us for all these years. We couldn't have done it without you—and you're probably wishing we hadn't.

We love you, still,
Sonny, Draper, and Stan

A Note from the Editor

A lot has been made in recent years about the importance of telling the truth. Governments, businesses, churches, and sports heroes have all been under fire for bending, twisting, and spinning a story for a variety of temporal and eternal reasons. Do any of them tell the truth? Anytime?

Well, okay, maybe some of them . . . sometimes.

But don't you get tired of people telling you stories about stuff that you just know are not true?

Wouldn't it be great, if for once, a friend would come up to you and say, "Hey, let me tell you a lie." Wouldn't that be refreshing?

Well, we tried to do that with this book. But the more we researched Sonny's stories and the historical obscurities hidden in Draper's drawings, the more we were convinced that most of this stuff is actually true! At least we think so. It's true (honest), we had trouble deciding if this was a book of true tales or fabulously tall tales.

Then we hit on a solution—or rather, Sonny did. Sonny is always right about such things. He said, "Who cares? It's just a good story."

So consider this book a cool, refreshing breeze. Sit back and enjoy . . . or keep standing if you're in line somewhere . . . and get your smiles going.

Most of these stories (we think) are probably true. Far be it for my friends and yours—Sonny and Draper—to lie to you.

There! We're telling you right up front. While we are all fascinated by facts and obscurities of life and history, just remember, this isn't intended as something for the reference shelf. It's for the coffee table, the guest room, the waiting room, and—ah, if you must—that other room.

A Note from Sonny

This book is the result of curiosity. Of course, we all know curiosity killed the cat—but at least he died satisfied. It seems I've been curious for a great portion of my life. I've always wanted to know or been interested in the odd, the origins, the superstitions, the animals, the folklore, and the truth about things that really don't matter too much.

Some things made me laugh, some things made me shout, "Bah humbug!" But all were worth collecting. For instance, I wanted to know the meaning and the origination of:

- The phrase "the whole nine yards"?
- What use are men's nipples?
- Why do empty rooms get dusty?
- What the hell is LIMELIGHT that people are always standing in?
- Why is a dog's nose moist?

- Why are women's feet always cold?
- Why do men always stand with their backsides to the fireplace?
- What makes flatulence flame?

Ah, sweet mysteries of life.

Over the years, the collection of the strange, the humorous, and the useless grew. It's common knowledge that money is something that things run into—and people run out of—and money is what was offered, if some of these odd and interesting facts were put in short story form and read as "features" on our syndicated radio.

Great idea—and so it came to pass.

Over 750 of these fascinating stories were written and broadcast—which brings us back to this book. It was fun writing these stories, it was fun broadcasting these stories, and even more fun was the warm response to these stories.

It was difficult, though, to pick which of the stories should go into this book. Well, we picked a few of them, and all you have to do is enjoy them and maybe satisfy a little of your curiosity. The sole purpose of this collection of words and pictures is simply to entertain, to bring a smile, or to raise an eyebrow.

Let me suggest you take a little extra time and look closely at Draper's drawings—they're more than just cartoons, they're marvelous, for they give life to the page. They'll also put pep in your step, and zest in your vest—however, I'm not too sure they'll put life in your wife.

In any event, enjoy. You may learn so many unimportant, useless, but amusing facts that at parties ordinarily polite people will tend to roll their eyes and edge away.

Sometimes I'm asked, "Where'd you get the information and the tidbits on all these liars, lovers, and losers? Who'd you consult when you put these little groups of words together?"

Well, I really didn't consult, but I did read, and I did make notes, and the research included visits to the library, the Internet, and, of course, more than a couple dozen modern and not so modern tomes.

Much of the material just naturally fell into place, and as Oscar Levant once said, "It doesn't really matter who said it first, it's who gets credit for it last that counts."

In one book, Ronald Smith points out that throughout history people have borrowed and even improved on classic lines. For instance, Charles Darwin wasn't first with the "survival of the fittest"—it was Herbert Spencer.

And how well I remember Franklin Delano Roosevelt's "the only thing we have to fear is fear itself." But if you look closely at what old Henry David Thoreau wrote years earlier, you'll read that he said, "Nothing is so much to be feared, as fear." And even before Thoreau, Francis Bacon penned, "Nothing is terrible, except fear itself." And historic Michel de Montaigne beat them all with, "The thing I fear most, is fear."

And don't overlook that great inaugural

speech by John F. Kennedy when he borrowed from Kahlil Gibran, who asked, "Are you a politician asking what your country can do for you, or a zealous one asking what you can do for your country?"

On the lighter side, Rodney Dangerfield gets credit for the story of the fellow who got bad news from his doctor and said he wanted a second opinion. The doctor said, "OK, you're ugly, too." But the line really originated with old Henny Youngman.

While we're at it, think back to the old Roseanne Barr sitcom where she was quoted as saying that her noisy kids made it clear that she now knew "why some animals eat their young." That line brought big laughs and critical acclaim, but it was originally used in the film *Mildred Pierce* and spoken by Eve Arden.

There are even some modern-day lines and stories that can be traced back over 250 years, but oh well, enough of history. Time now to just be amazed and amused, not necessarily in that order, by this interesting collection.

COW-A-BUNGA!

Did Mrs. O'Leary's cow start the historic Chicago Fire? Well, it's probably a myth—no real cause of this great fire was ever determined, and chances are it never will be. The fire started shortly before nine o'clock on the evening of October 8, 1871, in a barn owned by Patrick O'Leary. For several weeks there had been a drought and the wooden buildings of Chicago were dry as tinder, and this, coupled with a strong southwest wind, caused the flames to spread rapidly. The fire raged for two days and two nights, 200 people died, and 17,500 buildings were completely destroyed. It seems that Mrs. O'Leary had milked her cow at the usual time earlier in the evening, but she and her husband were in bed at the time the fire broke out, but they weren't asleep because the neighbors were having a loud party. A kerosene lamp with a broken chimney was later found in the ashes of the burned barn, which suggested the story that the fire was started by a kerosene lantern kicked over by the cow that Mrs. O'Leary was milking. The story originated before the fire was out and spread around the world and persists even though the evidence was contradictory. Of course, the O'Learys denied the cow story. A reporter named Michael Ahern, who died in 1927, is the man who concocted the story. He said he invented it so that his report would be more interesting. Like many reporters he never let a few facts stand in the way of a good story.

RUB
RUB
RUB
HIS
HERS
NOSE AID
NOSE VIAGRA
SHAVE & A HAIRCUT 2 BITS
NORTH P.
HOME SWEET IGLOO

LOVE WILL FIND A WAY

It has been said that people in tropical regions have a much more active sex life than the people in the more northerly climes, and that the weather is really responsible for this hyperactivity. Is that true? Well, I personally think it is. Of course I've never heard of wild times in an igloo, although there once was a report of a super-sensual Eskimo party that wound up with 20 broken noses. Anyhow, a recent study on human sexuality conducted at the University of Bangkok in Thailand showed that the ideal temperature to make love in is 77 degrees Fahrenheit, and since most of the tropics have a mean temperature between 75 and 80 degrees, I'm inclined to agree with the study. Another interesting sidelight to this research was the fact that the visual impact of lightly clad females anywhere excited the male's basic visceral drives a little more than somewhat. An anonymous doggerel writer put it this way:

The temperature may be zero,
It may be a horrible day,
But you can be sure, my friends,
That love will find a way!

THIS IS ABSURD—
WHOEVER HEARD
OF PENGUINS AT
THE NORTH POLE?

AHOY AND GOODBYE

Have you ever wondered why we say "Hello" when we answer the telephone? Why not "What's up, baby?" or "Go ahead, I'm listening," or even "I hear you calling, talk to me, talk to me." Well, we're told that when the very first telephone switchboard-and-exchange was installed in New Haven, Connecticut, way back in 1878, the salutation was a nautical term—"Ahoy! Ahoy!" which according to the history books was originally the war cry of the militant Vikings (no, not the Minnesota Vikings). Anyhow, that greeting was used for a couple of years, and then the British, always so polite, when they picked up the receiver used the phrase, "Are you ready to talk?" which became "Are you there?" The greeting "Are you there?" persisted for several years until folks started answering, "Of course, I'm here, you silly goose. Who'd you suppose answered the phone?" Then, so the story goes, one day Thomas Alva Edison picked up the receiver of a telephone and said "Hello" and thereby became the first person to use that word as an answer to the ring. The word at once became popular and has been used ever since. An interesting sidelight is that in 1941 the U.S. War Department ordered all its employees when answering interdepartmental calls to give their names instead of saying "Hello." They said it saved time. Isn't that interesting? What do you think? That's what I thought.

4

STORK LEGEND

There's a story going 'round that tells of the little five-year-old who asked his mother if it was true that the stork brought him. "Yes," said his harried mother. Then he asked if she was brought by the stork, and if Grandma was also brought by the stork. And when she had haltingly answered "yes" to those questions, the five-year-old just sighed and observed that there hadn't been any sex in the family for the past three generations. Well, where did the legend of storks bringing babies originate, anyway? The legend originated in northwestern Europe where the long-legged bird is regarded with a feeling bordering on reverence. In Roman mythology the stork was sacred to Venus, the goddess of love, and whenever a pair of storks built their nest on a housetop the ancients regarded it as a sign of Venus's blessing on the family. In Germany and the Netherlands, the stork signifies good luck. The superstition that the stork is a bringer of babies actually began several centuries ago, when even then it was easier for parents to blame the birds and bees and storks than to take a stand on sex education. In any event, the regal stork on the house remains the herald of a new birth, the guardian of the home, and the symbol of good luck.

What has the head like a horse, an external skeleton like an insect, a grasping tail like a monkey, eyes that can be moved independently like a chameleon's, and a pouch for carrying its offspring like a kangaroo? It would be a pretty wild beast—and I wouldn't blame you if you said that there is no such thing. Ah, but there is and we call it the seahorse. There are about 50 species of this interesting fish ranging in size from one to 12 inches in length. Actually, they look like dignified chess pieces as they move about with all the speed of a snockered snail, vibrating their transparent fins about 35 times a second. But the most interesting fact about these gentle, upright little saltwater swimmers is that it's the male who has the babies. It's poppa who actually carries and nurtures the young until birth. Which means the female seahorse finally realizes the dream of every mother since the beginning of time. You see, momma seahorse deposits the eggs in the special pouch that the male has on his belly. The pouch is sealed, fertilization takes place, and 45 days later 150 baby seahorses gallop out. They're off!

EAT YOUR SPINACH, KID!

Some long-ago comic once said, "This'd be a better world for spinach if the mothers ate the children." The line was inspired by the appearance in the 1930s by a new comic strip—Popeye the Sailorman. The silly-looking, knobby-kneed, lantern-jawed character with the funny-looking forearms got his mighty strength by consuming an inordinate amount of spinach. The amazing thing about this comic strip is that after it became popular, spinach consumption in the United States rose by an unbelievable 33 percent. Popeye got his overpowering strength because the leafy-green, blah-tasting vegetable contains great amounts of iron. Ah, but here's the mistake. The belief that spinach promotes strength was based on a mathematical error. You see, long ago nutrition researchers put a decimal point in the wrong place, which gave spinach ten times more iron than it actually contains! Some mistake—and the poor kids have suffered since. Its iron content is only average, and the little iron it does have is virtually ineffective because the body cannot absorb it directly. Makes you wonder about broccoli, doesn't it? Ah well, it's difficult to say anything nice about spinach, except that there're no bones in it.

IMMOVABLE MEETS IRRESISTIBLE

If you're interested in intellectual gobbledygook or scientific double-talk, listen to this. What would happen if an irresistible force met an immovable object? In the first place, according to all known laws of matter and energy, this condition could never happen. You see, if a force is "irresistible" it'll move an object in its path; or, in other words, there can be no immovable object with respect to an irresistible force. On the other hand, if an object is "immovable," no force can move it; which is another way of saying that there is no irresistible force with respect to an immovable object. And since the existence of the two conditions cannot take place at the same time, it is impossible to say what would happen if they did exist. The scientific nitpickers say you just cannot conceive of an irresistible force meeting an immovable object any more than you can conceive of two men, each one taller than the other. However, I can still remember an old girlfriend's definition when she said, "When an immovable object meets an irresistible force—somebody goes home early!"

MOONSTRUCK

In saloons, hospital emergency rooms, and police stations, they say that things really get crazy when the moon is full. Is there such a thing as "lunar effect" in susceptible human beings? Lots of folks believe there is. Years of research on this age-old belief shows there's really not much to hang this old wives' tale on. Nonetheless, many people remain convinced that the moon must do *something*. After all, the earth's surface is 75 percent water, and we all know about the tides. The human body is 75 percent water, so why shouldn't there be a human tidal effect? The big problem with this reasoning is the failure to take the question of size into account. The tides are only noticeable in the oceans; in smaller bodies of water, like lakes, tides are negligible, so you can imagine how little the influence the moon's gravitational pull has on the human body—less than negligible. So how do we explain all those bartenders, cops, and nurses who believe in the "lunar effect"? That's not too difficult, for you see, nobody seems to notice when there's a full moon and nothing happens—you only notice that when there's a full moon and something does happen. In other words, heads you win, tails doesn't count.

TELL THE POLICE COMMISSIONER THAT MY GIRL FRIENDS AND I HAVE HAD IT WITH THESE NIGHTLY INTRUSIONS

SON-OF-A-GUN

Well, I'll be a son-of-a-gun! How many times have you heard this expression? Probably less than a million. Do you have any idea where it comes from? Well, it comes from the early days of British sea power. Way back then, the sailing ships left port and stayed at sea for two or three years at a time. But the admirals had more common sense than we give them credit for, and sometimes allowed women to sail with the men, which seems like a pretty good arrangement to me. And, on long voyages, as you might suspect, there was an occasional baby born at sea. Obviously in those early vessels there wasn't much room for an infirmary or hospital room, and so when these tiny miracles occurred, the ship's surgeon usually delivered the child in a screened-off section of the gun deck, which meant the birth took place "under the gun." The infant commonly slept in a small hammock slung from a gun barrel. And, if the father of the child was unknown, then the entry in the ship's log read, "son-of-a-gun"—and that's how this phrase began. Nope, there's no record of a "daughter-of-a-gun" ever being born.

BELIEVE IT OR NOT!

Did you ever wonder where the phrase "believe it or not" came from? Of course you do. It was Robert L. Ripley. But his name wasn't Robert, it was Leroy, who was a minor league baseball player who injured his arm while trying out with the New York Giants. Ah, what to do? Well, he got a job with the *New York Globe* as a sports cartoonist. The editors didn't think Leroy sounded macho enough, so they changed his name to Bob. Then, one day as a deadline approached and he didn't have a fresh look for a sports cartoon, he came up with the idea of drawing cartoons of seven athletes who had set records for hopping, broad jumping on ice, running backward, touching their foreheads with their tongues, and so on. He knew some folks would think he'd made up the strange records and so he titled the cartoon—you guessed it—"Believe It or Not!" The reader response was so great that Ripley continued the sports oddities and gradually expanded it to include any kind of oddity known to man. He even gets credit for making the "Star-Spangled Banner" our official national anthem by pointing out in one of his columns that it was never officially confirmed. Congress took note, voted, and it became official in 1931. Believe it or not!

LUCKY "7"

Back in 1929, a St. Louis businessman named Charles L. Grigg began marketing a new drink. He called it Bib-Label Lithiated Lemon-Lime Soda. Not a very catchy name, and his advertising slogan wasn't much better. The slogan: "Take the ouch out of grouch." The carbonated soda became a great success, especially after the dramatic stock market crash of 1929 and during the depression years that followed. Some say its success was due to one of its strange ingredients, a powerful drug known as lithium carbonate. It is a drug that can now only be purchased by prescription and is used to treat manic depressives. The lithium salts seemed to have a calming effect on those who drank this new lemon-lime soda. Then they discovered that lithium could have some harmful effects on heart and kidney patients and so the drug was removed from the popular drink. They reduced the amount of carbonation and decided to change the name from the unwieldy Bib-Label Lithiated Lemon-Lime Soda to something a little easier to say. Since the drink originally came in a seven-ounce bottle and folks used to say "bottoms up" when they drank it, the name was changed to 7-Up. And that's where it stands today—refreshing. And in many cases it probably still takes the "ouch out of grouch."

CLOSE SHAVE

How did the barber pole originate? That's an easy one. The barber pole with spiral stripes is a relic of the days when barbers were also surgeons. As early as the fifth century, the barbers in Rome pulled teeth, treated wounds, and bled patients as part of their professional work. The barber-surgeons generally bled their patients in the arm, and, in the days when few people could read, pictures and emblems were used as shop signs. The emblem of the profession was a spirally painted white and red pole from which was suspended a brass basin with a semi-circular opening in the rim.

The white represented the bandage used in bloodletting, the red stripe represented the blood, and the basin represented the vessel used to receive the blood. In the United States the brass basin is omitted from the barber pole, but it's still common in Britain. American barbers also added a blue stripe just to make the colors conform to our flag. And when you consider how much a barber charges for a haircut nowadays, maybe they should add a green stripe as well—to represent money, of course.

THE RING THAT BINDS

Cynics say that "marriage is a romantic story in which the hero dies in the first chapter." Well, marriage is many things to many people, but almost all marriages seem to have one thing in common—the wedding ring. Historians agree that the custom of the wedding ring originated in Egypt in 2800 BC. The significance of the gold band, however, isn't too well defined. Some say that the ring was a symbol dating back to the barbarians who used a ring to chain their brides to their homes. Ancient Egyptians felt that the finger ring was a circle with no beginning and no end, and therefore signified eternity, which is how long a happy marriage is supposed to last. Two-thousand-year-old wedding rings of gold were unearthed at Pompeii and surprisingly were just like the friendship rings of today—that is, two carved hands clasped in a handshake. Some ancient rings had a miniature key welded to one side, which wasn't the key to a husband's heart, but symbolized the key to half the family treasury. They even found rings of iron. It seems that early Roman housewives wore them at home, but in public they switched and proudly wore a gold band. And is it really true that ring on the finger is worth two on the phone? Which proves opportunity knocks for every man, but a woman gets a ring!

BRING HOME THE BACON

Way back in the 12th century a marriage custom was started that lasted well into the 19th century and was responsible for an expression we still use today: "bringing home the bacon." Nowadays bringing home the bacon means returning with a victory or bringing home the cash. But back in the 12th century it actually meant bringing home a side of bacon. It all began at the church of Dunmow, in Essex County, England, where a flitch of bacon was awarded annually to the husband and wife who proved that they'd lived together in greater harmony and fidelity than any other competing couple. Who did the judging way back in the 12th century isn't clearly known, but by the 16th century there is evidence that a jury of six bachelors and six unmarried maidens judged the competing couples by questioning them closely. Just why bachelors and maidens did the judging doesn't make too much sense, although they know that it really takes two to make a marriage—a young girl and an anxious mother. In any event, the couple giving the most satisfactory answers were declared winners and given a year's supply of the prized pork, which they, of course, brought home. And with the price of bacon today, that's a pretty good prize to bring home.

HARD-HEARTED HICKORY

Andrew Jackson was our 17th president and had the nickname "Old Hickory." Hickory is tough and so was old Andy. Not only was he the first president to ride a train, but he was also the first president to ever marry a divorcée. Her name was Rachel Donelson and she figured in one of the most celebrated duels in history.

Way back when dueling was considered a much more satisfactory way to answer an insult than merely a lot of name-calling, you had to be careful what you said or who you said it to. Well, a fellow named Charlie Dickenson made a nasty remark about President Andrew Jackson's wife. You see, Rachel Donelson had married Andy thinking that her divorce was final. It wasn't, and so on a technicality they weren't really married. Of course, they had a second ceremony, but in the meantime they had committed adultery, and Andy didn't like to be reminded of it. Charlie Dickenson reminded him. Old Hickory replied by challenging Dickenson to a duel with pistols. Nothing too new for Andrew Jackson, as he'd had over 100 duels before he became our 17th president, which made his job as president seem like a visit to Toys "R" Us.

The 1806 duel took place at Harrison's Mills, Kentucky. Charlie fired first. Andy fired second. Charlie died that night, and President Andrew Jackson had a bullet in his chest that was too close to his heart to be removed; he carried it for the rest of his life. You might call the entire incident an affair of the heart.

THE CULTURED THIEF

Back in 1925 there was a detail in a crime that had authorities baffled until an informed jeweler gave them the answer. The crime deals with a jewel thief named Arthur Barry, who was really big-time back in the 1920s. He averaged close to half a million dollars in thefts a year. In today's money, that would be about four million dollars—almost as much as a .220 hitter gets. Anyhow, Arthur Barry made his way into a room in the posh Plaza Hotel in New York and stole more than $750,000 in jewels. Among the gems stolen was a string of pearls valued at $450,000. And here's the small mystery. In that same pilfered jewel box were four other strings of pearls that he didn't take. These four were imitations, imitations it was said that were so good they'd have fooled an oyster. Was Arthur Barry's choice pure luck? How'd he know which string of pearls to take and which to leave? Easy. You see, he simply rubbed the pearls gently across his teeth. Fake pearls are smooth and slippery, but real pearls give a slightly rough, grating sensation, and that's how he knew. The thief was caught and the pearls returned, which proves that crime doesn't pay, but the hours are good.

CRIME DOESN'T PAY—WELL

In the annals of crime, names like the Boston Strangler and Jack the Ripper are, unfortunately, well-known. Well, now I think you can add one more name. Not as well-known and certainly not as fascinating, but one that bears remembering when you're in need of a smile. Call him "The Connecticut Dummy," one of the world's dumbest robbers. Here's what happened near Brookfield, Connecticut, in 1985. A hitchhiker, James Galen, was picked up by a sympathetic and unwary motorist. A few minutes of conversation and the hitchhiker made his move. He punched the driver in the nose, stole his wallet, and then ordered him to stop in downtown Brookfield, where Galen calmly got out and slowly sauntered away. When the ungrateful hitchhiker got home, he not only found that the wallet he'd stolen was empty, but he also found that he'd left his own wallet, containing $70, in the victim's car. What's he do? He simply picked up the phone, called his victim, and offered to exchange wallets. Of course his victim agreed, set up a meeting, and naturally called the police. When the police arrested the stupid thief, they said that they half expected him to ask, "How'd you find me?" Indeed, the Connecticut Dummy.

LOOK A BOOK!

Jacob Schlossberg used to say that "the fountain of wisdom flows through books." He was right. Did you know that Theodore Roosevelt, 26th president of the United States, wrote 40 books? Or that General Lew Wallace's bestseller, *Ben-Hur,* published in 1880, was the first work of fiction ever blessed by a pope? It's also interesting to know that Clement Clarke Moore, a biblical scholar, professor of Oriental and Greek literature, and compiler of Hebrew lexicon, wrote the delightfully simple and easily remembered *Visit from St. Nicholas*—"'Twas the night before Christmas and all through the house . . ." And in the world of books, you'll have to smile when you read of a Dutch doctor and chemist who died in 1738 and left behind a sealed book with the engaging title, *The Onliest and Deepest Secrets of the Medical Art.* The book, still sealed, was auctioned off for over $20,000! When the new owner broke the seal, he found that 99 of the 100 pages were blank! Only the title page had a handwritten note by the author. It said: "Keep your head cool, your feet warm, and you'll make the best doctor poor!" Ain't that the truth?

A CAVEMAN'S BEST FRIEND

You've probably seen cartoons of a prehistoric caveman dragging a hapless woman by the hair out of a cave and across the landscape-primeval for whatever purposes cavemen had for women. Smile if you will, but that's the beginning of the custom known as "having the best man at the wedding." Why do we have a best man at weddings? Well, when this primitive marriage-by-capture took place, the groom naturally, under those circumstances, would choose a faithful friend or follower to go with him to help fight off the attacks of the girl's relatives while he stole away with her. So, you see, the appearance of the bridegroom with his chief "best man" at the bride's home really represents a prehistoric raiding expedition. The term "best man" is of Scottish origin, and, according to the Oxford dictionary, dates back to about 1814. And what about the bridesmaid? Bridesmaids symbolize the female attendants or "girl friends" who used to help, or pretended to help, defend the bride against her abductors. And, as some smart alecks say, always get married at noon. That way if the marriage doesn't work out, you haven't ruined the whole day!

THE CLEVER CONE

You scream, I scream, we all scream for ice cream. And that's true, because ice cream is America's favorite dessert. Annual production comes to fifteen quarts a year for every man, woman, and child in the United States. Who invented it? Surprisingly, it was the Chinese, 4,000 years ago. However, the first and extremely popular delicacy was more like a pasty milk ice than smooth ice cream. Now who invented the ice cream cone? For centuries ice cream was served in saucers and dishes, and heaped on top of waffles. Then in 1904 at the St. Louis World's Fair, there were two concession stands next to each other. One was run by a waffle maker, the other by an ice cream vendor, and together they changed America's dessert habit. The ice cream vendor ran out of paper dishes and, in desperation, rolled one of the nearby waffles into a cone. Voilà! A sensation was born.

The newspapers call this new combination "World's Fair Cornucopias." Soon blobs of ice cream atop the cone became as commonplace as cornstalks in Kansas. The cones were rolled by hand until 1912. Then an enterprising American inventor from Portland, Oregon, named Fred Bruckman patented a machine for doing the job. And the rest, as they say, is history. I like pistachio on a sugar cone. How about you?

HOT TONGUE AND COLD SHOULDER

Where do you suppose the expression "giving someone the cold shoulder" originated? Well, near as we can determine, it started a long time ago in medieval France during the Dark Ages when men were men and women were women—which was a pretty good arrangement at that. In those days it was the custom when guests arrived to invite them to dinner, to slake their thirst, and to give them time to rest. It was also the custom of the times to serve hot roasts. Now, if the guests outstayed their welcome, or made themselves a little obnoxious to the host, a cold shoulder of mutton or beef was served instead of the customary hot meal. In other words, the guest was given the "cold shoulder"—a subtle and direct way of saying, "You've worn out your welcome, Mac, hit the road!" Of course, some historians say that the phrase is the outgrowth of actually keeping the back or at least one shoulder between them and a person they dislike. Personally, I like the mutton and beef story better, just seems to make more sense. And 50 million Frenchmen can't be wrong—right?

MANDIBULAR MAGIC

Back in 1893, the White House kept one of the biggest secrets in presidential history. The rumor was that the president of the United States, Grover Cleveland, underwent a secret operation for the removal of his upper jaw. The strange thing is that the rumor was absolutely true! But the doctors who'd performed the difficult operation kept it a secret for almost twenty-five years. In June 1893 a malignant ulcer was discovered on the roof of the president's mouth. A one-month vacation was quickly announced, and President Cleveland went by train to New York and then aboard a friend's yacht. As they steamed up the East River, a team of doctors removed Cleveland's entire upper left jaw! While he recuperated an artificial rubber jaw was made. The papers ran wild with stories of the operation and the rumors continued, and, as usual, they were vehemently denied. Three months after the serious surgery, President Cleveland silenced all the talk by giving a rousing speech. Scores of reporters on hand failed to notice anything out of the ordinary—a tribute to the good fit of the artificial jaw. In 1917, twenty-five years after the operation, one of the surgeons finally revealed the truth. Who says you can't keep a secret in Washington where sound travels faster than light?

CLASSIFIED CONFIDENTIAL

I'VE GOT A SECRET...

PILTDOWN MAN*

* See SUSSEX, England c. 1909

PIE IN THE SKY

In 1870, a man named William Russell Frisbie opened the Frisbie Pie Company in Bridgeport, Connecticut, not far from the Yale University campus. Frisbie pies were homemade in circular tin pans stamped with the family name. In the mid-1940s, Yale students used to relax by sailing those pie plates as a lawn game. Nobody paid much attention to this little-known sport until a Californian by the name of William Morrison, who was nuts about UFOs, thought he could make a buck on America's craze for flying saucers. So he went to the Wham-O toy company, where they devised for him a toy disc whose shape and movement, when sailed through the air, mimicked the flying saucers that Hollywood had popularized in those "outer space" movies. The president of Wham-O toys then went on a promotional tour with the new saucer toy. When he got to the eastern college campuses, he was astounded that students of Yale and Harvard were playing a game with metal pie tins that students called Frisbies, from the name stamped on the bottom of the pie plate. He liked the name, didn't even know about the Frisbie Pie Company, and in 1957 trademarked the word *Frisbee*. And that's how it got its name—from pie in the sky to money-maker in America.

WISE FLYERS

One of the most fascinating harbingers of the changing seasons is the flight of migratory geese—south in the fall and north in the spring. Why do you suppose that wild geese fly in a V-shaped formation? No, it's not because the leader reduces the wind force for the entire flock. It's the opposite that's true. A certain amount of wind is necessary to the sustained flight of birds. Not only that, but flying in wedge-shaped formation enables each bird to avoid the wake of the bird up ahead. Flying in V-formation also makes it easier for each bird in the flock to see the leader more clearly. Observers of wild geese and ducks note that when the wind blows strongly from one side, sort of like a crosswind, one side of the V is longer than the other. Sometimes when the crosswind is extremely strong, they abandon the V formation and fly single file. You see, the wedge formation really doesn't reduce the wind resistance for the flock at all. Incidentally, geese mate for life and mama and papa and the little goslings stay together during the migration and the following winter. When spring comes the older birds drive the young away to let them make their own mistakes. So, how come they're called *silly* geese?

FEET HURT BUT NOSES RUN

There's a great deal of difference between knowing and understanding. You can know a lot about something and not really understand it. For instance, you may know a great deal about animals. You may know whether or not carp have to wear aqua-lungs in polluted water, and you may know whether or not an armadillo can be peeled, but do you know why your nose runs in the cold, cold of winter? Well, according to a slender, graying surgeon named Jonathan Finley, the cold air is inhaled, and when it hits the mucous membranes inside the nose, the imbedded capillaries constrict.

Then, after a short period of constriction, the capillaries change their minds and dilate. During this dilation the blood slows down, and the blood cells of the blood vessels become more fluid, which in turn allows the mucous glands to drip a little serum. And that's all there is to it. So you see, the lip can slip, the eye can lie, but the nose knows. And as we all know, plastic surgeons can do almost anything with a nose, except keep it out of other people's business. Then there's the story of the little boy who once took his nose apart just to see what made it run. Ho-ho-ho! And now I've got to run!

CRYABILITY

If at first you don't succeed, cry, cry again! And let those tears flow. As we all know, tears clean and lubricate the eye and help prevent infection. Well, lately there's been a great deal of research on those salty little drops of water, with some interesting discoveries. One of the things scientists wanted to know was whether the tears we shed when we're upset differ from the tears that flow when we peel onions. The answer is yes. There's a chemical difference. They found that in the two groups of tears, the emotional and the onion-inspired, the emotional tears contained much larger amounts of proteins. In addition to the protein discovery, researchers found that there are toxic substances that accumulate in the body as a result of stress, and tears help flush them out! Which, perhaps, explains why we sometimes feel better after a good cry. And since there's a great similarity between blood and tears, many in the scientific field believe that analyzing tears could be just as valuable as analyzing blood. The one thing that all men seem to agree on, however, is the fact that women's tears are the greatest waterpower known to man.

CREEPY, CRAWLY FORECASTERS

Many people believe that animals and insects can foretell the kind of weather we'll get, as evidenced by the great belief that the wooly bear caterpillar predicts the kind of winter we'll have. It's a problem, all right, knowing just what to believe. Well, I personally think the biggest problem nowadays is which wine to serve with Twinkies. As for the wooly bear, well, a study at the American Museum of Natural History in New York proved that there's as much truth in this age-old superstition as there is in a pot of gold at the end of the rainbow.

Maybe you still believe that leprechauns make shoes and that babies are found under cabbage leaves. That's up to you. However, if you want to, you can believe that if the brown bands of stripes around the caterpillar are wide, we'll have a mild winter. If they're narrow, we'll have a wild and wooly winter coming up. As for me, I don't believe in superstition. It's bad luck. And I especially don't believe in a wooly bear caterpillar that's not really made of wool, that's not really a bear, and that's only a caterpillar—temporarily.

WHITHER THE WEATHER?

"Everybody talks about the weather, but nobody does anything about it!" Who made that original statement? Was it really Mark Twain? The answer is no, it wasn't Mark Twain. Way back in 1890, even before there was an icicle built for two, a newspaper editor for the *Hartford Courant,* in an editorial, made the now-famous, overused, and attributed-to-the-wrong-man statement. The editor's name was Charles Dudley Warner, and I think it's about time we gave Mr. Warner credit for the original line. However, what Mark Twain did say about the weather was that it was "a literary specialty and no untrained hand can turn out a good article on it." Maybe so. Author Bill Nye once said, "Winter lingered so long in the lap of Spring that it occasioned a great deal of talk." While one of the most fitting and weather-wise quotations was made by the pixieish Don Marquis, who said, "Don't cuss the climate—it probably doesn't like you any better than you like it." So remember, don't knock the weather. Without it, how would we start conversations?

BARTLEY AND THE WHALE

It is rumored that Jonah said to the whale, "If you hadn't opened your big mouth I wouldn't be in this fix." Well, maybe he did. Anyhow, is it possible for a man to be swallowed by a whale and live? They say it actually happened to a young sailor on a whaling ship in 1891. An 80-foot-long sperm whale was sighted in the south Atlantic. The boats were sent out, and a young harpooner named James Bartley sent his harpoon into the side of the 80-foot beast. The whale dived, his flukes slamming the water and capsizing the boats. The whale was finally killed, but two crewmen were missing. The carcass was pulled alongside the mother ship and processing began. When they got to the stomach of the beast they noticed movement inside. When it was opened Bartley was discovered unconscious. They revived him, but he wasn't rational and so they confined him to the captain's quarters for two weeks. Within four weeks he'd recovered enough to tell what it had been like to live in the belly of a whale. He remembered the boat being slammed, then complete darkness, as he slipped along a smooth passage. Everything was slimy and the heat was unbearable. The next thing he knew he was in the captain's cabin. For the rest of his life Bartley's face, hands, and neck remained stark white—bleached by the whale's gastric juices. And that's a whale of a tale.

RUST-OLEUM ANYONE?

They say you are what you eat. And if that's true then a fellow named Michael Lotito, from Grenoble, France, could be a hardware store. You see, Messr. Lotito has an act wherein he eats metal and glass and almost anything you can imagine. His stage name is Monsieur Mangetout which is French for Mr. Eat It All. His strange act actually began when he was a child. Kids teased him because he was sickly and suffered from rickets, and so to win their admiration and prove his resistance to pain, he chewed glass and stuck needles into his body. From this he developed his unique act. His eating performances are legendary. He's chewed his way through supermarket carts, TV sets, aluminum skis, and several bicycles, to say nothing about hundreds of razor blades, plates, bottles, bullets, bolts, and phonograph records. Over a two-year period he even ate an airplane, a Cessna 150. Lotito's technique is to first cut the objects into bite-size portions, lubricate his digestive tract with mineral oil, and drink great amounts of water while eating. Disbelieving doctors have found that part of what he eats is broken down by his unusually strong digestive juices, and that the lining of his stomach and intestines are twice as thick as average. As a result he can eat metal and other apparently indigestible objects, but ironically he has trouble with soft stuff, like eggs and bananas. One thing we're sure of is that he has enough iron in his system.

BARN BUDDIES

How did the expression "get your goat" originate? Of course, you know the meaning—to annoy, irritate, or make someone angry. Well, some folks say it refers to the chin-tuft of hair on a goat, and the beard that some people wear resembles this chin-tuft—a goatee. The phrase, therefore, must just mean pulling one's beard, which, like tweaking the nose, is considered a humiliating insult or "getting one's goat." That's simple and direct, but just not true. It actually comes from horse breeders in the early days of horse racing. It was a well-known fact that thoroughbred horses often form loose attachments to goats. So, goats were often put in the stall of a nervous and high-strung racehorse to keep it company. Sometimes a horse and a goat became so inseparable that the horse would become nervous and restive when the goat was taken away. And sometimes, the more unscrupulous horse trainers, in the still of the night, would come and steal the goat, leaving the horse in a terrible state of anxiety, giving someone the edge in the day's race. And if you've got a few bob on the bang-tailed nag, it's enough to "get your goat."

THE WHOLE NINE YARDS

There are some mysteries of the ages—like: Why is the Mona Lisa smiling her secret smile? What is the riddle of the sphinx? How long is a piece of string? How high is up? But the mystery of just where the expression "the whole nine yards" comes from currently tops the list. No one really seems to know. For instance, some say the expression comes from the nautical term "yard," meaning the nine yardarms on a square-rigged sailing ship. Others say that coal trucks originally held nine cubic yards of coal, and, in anticipation of a hard winter, you asked for the whole nine yards. Then there are those who say the phrase comes from ready-mix concrete trucks that allegedly held nine cubic yards of concrete. Some say tailors use exactly nine square yards of material to make a man's three-piece suit. Then there are those who maintain that it comes from the olden days when a first-class bridal veil was nine yards in length. Finally, undertakers, the last ones to let you down, say the mysterious expression comes from the belief that a burial shroud was made out of a whole nine yards of cloth. In any event no one seems to know the truth. And the truth, as we all know, is sometimes stranger than fish stories.

OF MICE AND MEN, AND ONE SILENT NIGHT

The year was 1818, the place was a little town in Austria named Oberndorf, the time was Christmas Eve, and the church was preparing for Christmas Eve Mass. When they tested the organ they found that mice had eaten holes in the bellows and the organ wasn't playable. What to do? A silent organ needed quick repairs and so they sent for the organ repairman who wasn't due in town for a couple of months, and music was indeed needed for the Mass. The organist, a man named Franz Gruber, found a poem written by a priest named Josef Mohr, and set about composing music for the poem. It took him three and a half hours. The song began, "Stille Nacht, Heilige Nacht," or "Silent Night, Holy Night." That night the priest and the organist sang their composition accompanied by a guitar and a children's choir and the song was an immediate hit. Months later when the organ repairman finally showed up, Gruber gave him a copy of the song, which he circulated widely in his travels. The song caught on and was billed on all programs as a folk song by "authors unknown." Time went skidding by, and by 1854 the song was attributed to several famous composers, including the son of Josef Haydn. Then in 1854, quite by accident, a choir director happened to ask a student for a copy of the song. The student turned out to be the son of Franz Gruber, the organist, and suddenly (36 years late) the true composer of this famous song was credited with its writing. It took 36 years, but at least it's nice to know the truth.

Do mice ever sing? A strange question. But some mice actually do sing, making musical sounds that sound like the twittering, chirping, whistling, or warbling of small birds. Even some ordinary species of house mice sing up a storm. Dozens of competent authorities investigated this little-known phenomenon and say it's true, although some scientists say that the noise is the result of some obstruction in their bronchial tubes. In other words, the singing is merely a whistling sound made by mice that have caught cold and are having trouble breathing. I've had some trouble myself. Then

Roy Chapman Andrews, of the American Museum of Natural History, reported that a singing mouse observed by him in China actually uttered musical chirps, birdlike in quality that varied in notes and tones. He said it was definitely a song like that of a bird and was not caused by the inflammation of the respiratory tract. You don't suppose that Walt Disney knew this long before the so-called authorities, do you? Probably. I even heard of a mouse that ran away from home when he discovered his father was a rat.

HOBSON'S CHOICE IS NO CHOICE

There's an old pitch-man's line that goes, "You pays your money you gets your choice." But what if you get no choice at all? What do you call that? The answer is—Hobson's choice. How did this expression enter our language anyhow? Well, it all started back in the 16th century in Cambridge, England, where a man named Tobias Hobson ran a livery stable. He was a no-nonsense kind of guy who wouldn't take any guff from the smart-aleck college kids when they came in to rent a horse from him. They'd come in and demand a horse of another color, or a fast horse, or a horse that was best looking or smartest. Well, Mr. Hobson had other ideas. He told each customer that he must take the horse closest to the stable door. As the horse went out, old Hobson would rotate the remaining horses, and the next customer would then again get the one by the door. Every renter was treated the same, and the students started calling the practice Hobson's choice, meaning that no matter what they wanted they were given the horse that Mr. Hobson wanted to saddle up. The students began referring to any forced choice, whether it be girl, book, or horse—as Hobson's choice.

EXPLOSIVE HEADACHE

Phineas P. Gage, a man with a headache that's listed in the annals of medicine and known as the American Crowbar Case, has baffled doctors for generations. An amazing story. You see, Phineas Gage was a 25-year-old foreman, working on the construction of a railroad in Cavendish, Vermont, on September 13, 1848. He was preparing a charge of dynamite with a 13-pound crowbar when he accidentally triggered the charge. The explosion drove the three-foot-long crowbar through his brain and out the top of his head, leaving a large hole. His horrified co-workers picked him up, took him to a hotel a mile away, and miraculously, with just a little help, he walked up two flights of stairs, where a couple of doctors cleansed the wound. He never lost consciousness. Within two months he recovered enough to go home, although he did lose the sight in one eye and suffered periods of delirium. Within three months he was back on the job and seemed relatively normal for several years. He died in 1861. Hard to believe that he lived 13 years with a three-and-a-half-inch hole in his skull. His skull is on display at the Harvard medical school—probably right next to the bottle of aspirin.

THERE'S NO BUSINESS LIKE SNOW BUSINESS

During the winter months in North American climes, snowplows and salt seem to be the weapons for combating slippery streets. Have you ever wondered if they always used this equipment or was there an old-fashioned way to handle the buildup of snow? In the old days, when it snowed, cities just let it snow, and then let it lay there until warmer weather returned. Up until about 1920 we poor humans didn't do much about winter snow and ice, just sort of trudged along as well as we could. Then some smart ironmonger hammered out a blade, called it a snowplow, and had it drawn by horses, or attached it to the front of early-model trucks. From 1880 until the snowplows, however, the snow roller was used quite extensively. A snow roller was a huge, heavy drum, six feet in diameter and ten feet across, that was pulled by teams of horses through the streets packing down the snow to a hard surface. This allowed the runners on the sleigh a quicker and slicker surface over which the horses skidded down the frozen streets—which is still better than today's salt or chemicals that can quickly eat through the frame of the family flivver or having three little old ladies with tablespoons and large baggies in charge of snow removal, which seems to be the case in most large cities today.

Some people define "news" as the same old thing happening to different people. But just where did the word *news* originate? Well, it's a popular misconception that the word comes from the four cardinal points of the compass. The claim was that before the advent of news-papers, stories about recent events of general interest were posted in public places under four columns headed N*E*W*S. Happenings in the north recorded under N, those from the east under E, and so on. However, that theory is without foundation. You see, "news" is merely the plural of "new" and originally meant "new things." For instance, back in the 14th century the word was written one of three ways: newes, newis, and newys and was pronounced in two syllables. The Latin form of the word was nova, and the Anglo-Saxon spelling was niwi. Both forms meant "new things," recent, or fresh. Undoubtedly, some are probably wondering if "news" is singular or plural? But it doesn't really matter, does it? Just flip on the radio and hear the anchorman say, "The convicted murderer was granted a stay of execution, and will not be hanged." Or, "No noose is good noose."

FANCY YOUR PHILTRUM

Sometimes we don't know what's going on right under our noses. Take that little indentation between the nose and the upper lip. Believe it or smile, but that little concavity has a name. It's called the philtrum. Scientists can't agree on just what purpose this little canal serves, or if it has any purpose at all, but if you go way back several thousands of years, you'll find that the ancient Greeks considered this innocent little dent, the philtrum, one of the body's most erogenous zones. Perhaps that's why kissing is such a pleasurable activity. Wonder if you could get a ticket for overtime parking in an erogenous zone? And now that you know what a philtrum is, what do you know about something that we all have and sometimes lose? Hair. About the only thing that can really effect hair is fire. It's almost impossible to destroy. It decays at such a slow rate that it practically never disintegrates. Hair isn't affected by cold, a change of climate, water, or other natural forces. It's also resistant to many kinds of acids and corrosive chemicals, which is why it clogs sinks and drainpipes so easily. Now, if we could only keep it firmly anchored in our scalps. Ah, that's another story.

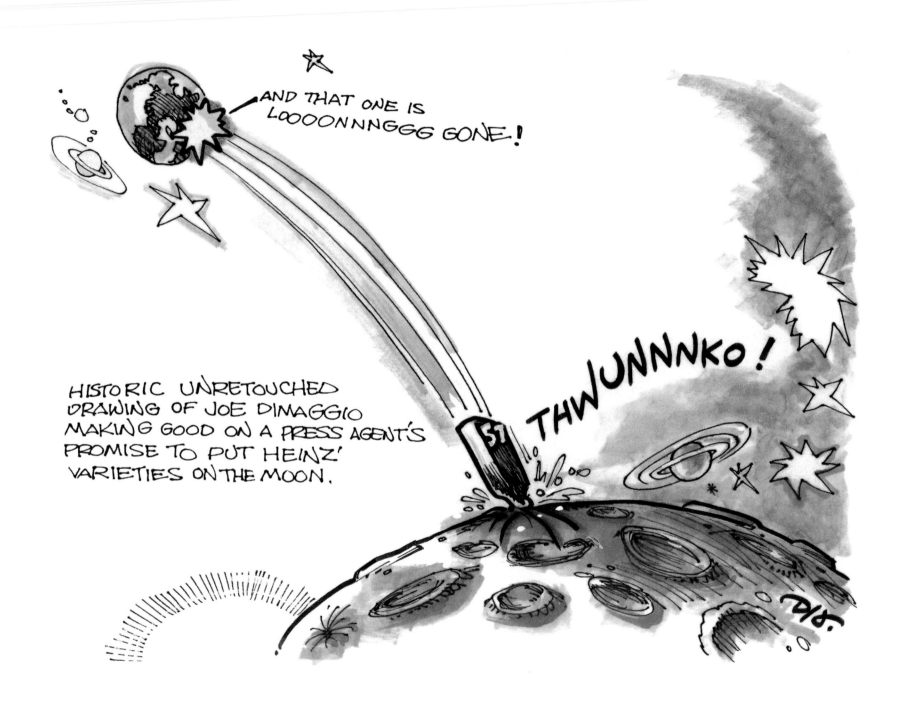

STREAK HITTER

Joltin' Joe DiMaggio is a symbol of a time now past. He was also one of the finest ballplayers in the history of the grand old national pastime. His grace, power, and consistency ensured his place in the Hall of Fame at Cooperstown. But did you know that he also loved to read Superman comic books? According to Lefty Gomez, the old Yankee pitcher, DiMaggio was afraid to buy them at the newsstands for fear of being recognized. And while everyone knows of his marriage to Marilyn Monroe, few know that his first wife was also a beautiful, blond Hollywood actress named Dorothy Arnold. After his first date with sex symbol Monroe the curious reporters asked Marilyn what she thought of the Yankee Clipper. "Well," she said, "you might say he 'struck out!'" However, the great hitter that he was, his next time at bat he must've hit a home run because they soon got married. His great hitting streak of 56 consecutive games in 1941 set a Major League record that doesn't look as though it'll ever be broken, and has an interesting sidelight. When DiMaggio's streak was broken, he lost $10,000 because the Heinz 57 people had a deal with him, ready to pay, when he reached 57 straight games. Which is something like inventing a soft drink called 6-Up.

DENSITY, SHMENSITY—IT'S A HOME RUN!

It's time we put to rest the opposing theories on whether a baseball will travel farther on a moist, muggy day than it will on a cool, dry day. Well, I always say that women will never make good umpires because they never think a man is safe—when he's out! I also say that a baseball can be hit farther on a humid day than a dry day, because contrary to popular belief, the addition of water vapor to the atmosphere reduces air density. The less density, the less hindrance to an object flying through the air and the greater distance you can hit a baseball—or a golf ball for that matter. As my old friend Red Jones, a former American League umpire, used to say, "On a cold day hitting a ball out of the park is like trying to throw a ripe strawberry through a battleship." You can decrease air density in four ways: by (1) increasing altitude, (2) raising the temperature, (3) lowering the barometric pressure, or (4) increasing the humidity. So if the Detroit Tigers want to hit home runs, they should play all their games at an elevation of 14,000 feet with the temperature at 90+ degrees, and the relative humidity at 95 percent. What a spot for a new stadium that would be!

ARE YOU IN GOOD HANDS WITH LLOYD'S OF LONDON?

How did Lloyd's of London get its name, and are they an insurance company? Lloyd's got its name in 1688 from a restaurant! A group of insurance underwriters used to meet in a London coffeehouse owned by a man named Edward Lloyd. 86 years later in 1774 they moved their meeting place to their present quarters in the Royal Exchange, and in 1871 they were incorporated by an act of Parliament. Lloyd's has over 1,800 members. One of the most widespread misconceptions is that Lloyd's is an insurance company. Not true. It's merely an insurance and business exchange, and each member, or underwriter, does business on his own account or in partnership with other members. The members, working in groups or "syndicates," write virtually every conceivable kind of insurance—except life insurance. All policies are written on a yearly basis, and gambling and betting by members is forbidden. Lloyd's, like a stock exchange, guarantees nothing. Only the members take the risk that is unlimited. All the association does is provide a meeting place and facilities for its members and sets the regulations that underwriters must live by—or die by—depending on the kind of insurance they have.

PEEPING TOM PEEPED

Phyllis Diller once said that if a peeping Tom ever peeped through her window, he'd reach in and pull the shades down himself. Well, just where did the expression "Peeping Tom" come from? The answer is that it dates way back to the Lady Godiva legend. You see, Lady Godiva was a most compassionate woman, and when her husband, the Lord of Coventry, imposed a burdensome tax on his subjects, the sympathetic Lady Godiva appealed to him to reconsider and cancel the obnoxious tax. "Fat chance," he said. However, he made a deal with his wife, saying that he'd cancel the tax if she would ride naked through the streets of Coventry. Lady Godiva took her husband at his word and issued a proclamation asking all persons to remain indoors and close the shutters while she rode through town clothed only in her long hair and chastity. Everybody complied. Well, almost everybody. Tom the tailor bored a hole in his shutter so he could see the curvaceous Lady Godiva pass. He got an eyeful, but because of his impudence, it is said, he was stricken blind. At any rate, he has been known as Peeping Tom ever since. And that's where the phrase comes from. Incidentally, the horse got home three hours before Lady Godiva, it says here.

MOMENTARY HOLINESS

Way back in time when the world was young, religious elders believed that a man's soul could be separated from his body by the evil machinations of Satan. If the soul was lost, then the devil moved in and took over the body, a condition certainly not to be desired. And so, as you might suspect, it was more essential for everyone to keep "body and soul" together. And that's where the oft-used expression comes from. You may just wonder how the devil got the souls to leave the body in the first place. What kind of cheating trickery did he use? Well, of course, there are many ways to lose one's soul, but one of the more common ways was simply by . . . sneezing! You see, some ancients actually believed that a sneeze would force the soul out of the body through the nostrils, and Satan himself, who obviously lurked everywhere, would take that minute opportunity to slip in and block the soul's return. Ah, but if a friend blessed you when you sneezed, then, because of your momentary holiness, the devil could not enter, and your soul could return to your body once again. And that, of course, is why we say "God bless you" when a person sneezes, or, as Humphrey Bogart once said, "here's looking ACHOO, kid."

LADY FINGERS!

What English queen had six fingers on one hand? It was Anne Boleyn, second wife of King Henry VIII. The sixth finger, however, was little more than a stump covered by a nail that turned up at the sides. Anne wore gloves whenever possible, but Queen Catherine used to get revenge on her rival by making Anne play cards—without gloves. King Henry, it is said, hated to look at this minor deformity. Maybe that had something to do with poor Anne losing her head, because King Henry soon tired of Anne Boleyn and the poor six-fingered sexpot was sent to the chopping block—which is getting rid of dandruff the hard way! And while we are speaking of hands, what is a dead man's hand in cards? Well, in poker, a hand consisting of a pair of aces and a pair of eights is known as a dead man's hand because those were the cards famed gunfighter Wild Bill Hickok was holding when he was shot by dangerous Jack McCall during a card game in Deadwood, South Dakota, in 1876. Some poker players claim that a dead man's hand is lucky and rarely beaten. Not me. I'll take a royal flush every time.

STONED IN BLARNEY

What would you be, after kissing the blarney stone? And how did the legend come to be? Blarney Castle, in County Cork, Ireland, was built about 1446 and named after the little town of Blarney. And that's all it was, just a castle named Blarney. Then about 100 years later Queen Elizabeth appointed a nobleman to act as her agent and get all the castles and strongholds in the region to surrender peacefully and be part of the crown. The owner of Blarney Castle wasn't too pleased with this plan, but not wanting to appear completely rebellious, he sort of sweet-talked the queen's agent and delayed the surrender from month to month—and then from year to year until it became a laughing matter and "Blarney" became the byword for soft speech and light-hearted persuasiveness to gain an end. To commemorate the achievement they set a certain stone high up on the castle wall that was accessible only with great difficulty. Kissing the blarney stone, it was said, would give the kisser the gift of soft speech and good-humored persuasiveness that had stood the owner of the castle in such good stead so many years ago. And that's no blarney.

LEGENDARY NONSENSE

Ah, those urban legends—stories that are absolutely untrue but are always told as having actually happened to a friend, or a friend of a friend, or someone that my sister's best friend knows. Back in the 1950s and 1960s, the story that ran rampant was of the woman who thought she had the perfect hairdo, the "beehive," with which she was so pleased that she left it in place for an inordinate amount of time, spraying more and more hairspray, and neglecting to have it washed. She developed a terrific pain on the top of her head and wound up in the hospital. When the doctors took the hairdo apart, they discovered that a black widow spider had moved in and bitten her on the head. The poor woman died soon afterward. All baloney; it never happened! But folks still like to tell the story, swearing it's the gospel truth. There's another phony story that's so outrageous that common sense would make you smile in disbelief, but still the bizarre story persists. It's the one about a woman who fell asleep while sunbathing. An ant climbed into her nose and laid eggs in her nasal passages. The eggs hatched, the itching became unbearable, and she scratched the flesh right off her cheeks. Well, now you can scratch those stories right off your list.

A NOISY NOISE ANNOYS!

How many times have you heard the question, "If a tree should fall in a forest thousands of miles from any living creature, would any sound be produced?" The answer depends on the definition of sound. Now, ordinarily sound is defined as the sensation stimulated by air waves set in motion by a vibrating object. So there is no sound unless there is some kind of ear to receive the sensation. In this sense, if a tree should fall thousands of miles from any living creature, there is no sound. Ah, but that's only the psychological sense of the term. How about the physical science definition? Then sound is defined as the cause of the sensation, that is, the air waves which are set in motion by a vibrating object to produce that which is popularly called sound. And so the answer to the question is in two parts—in the psychological sense of the term, no sound is produced unless there's an ear to hear, but in the physical sense, sound is produced regardless of the presence of a living creature with auditory organs. Which, of course, means you can keep right on arguing in any sense you want.

IS THIS SOME KIND OF JOKE?

ECHO-CENTRIC

The word *echo* means the repetition of a sound caused by the reflection of sound waves. But in Greek mythology it has a much more romantic meaning. The myth has it that Zeus, chief of all Olympian gods, was somewhat of a womanizer, which made his wife, Hera, very, very jealous. She followed him wherever he went. Old Zeus tried to outwit her by having a nymph named Echo intercept her and keep her occupied while he went about "playing around." Hera saw through the trick and in a fit of rage used her magical powers to condemn the nymph to wander the earth and never speak unless someone had spoken first, and then to repeat only that which had been said. And so poor little Echo wandered long and mournfully over the hills. One day she saw the beautiful Narcissus admiring his reflection in a pool and fell madly in love with him. Of course, it was unrequited love. And so in sadness the poor nymph pined away, wasting away until nothing was left except her voice. And that's the voice we hear coming back in certain spots. We still call it "echo" in memory of a lovelorn nymph. And you thought it was just the reflection of sound waves.

MAN'S SECOND BEST FRIEND

They say that a man's best friend is his dog. But near the town of Port Elizabeth, South Africa, a man's best friend turned out to be, of all things, a baboon! The man was James Wide, who worked for the railroad. In 1877, in an unfortunate accident, Wide lost both his legs. When he recovered he was reassigned to a light job as a switchman in a remote railroad tower, where he settled down to a lonely life in a little cabin in the boondocks. Then, wonder of wonders, he made friends with an inquisitive baboon, whom he named Jack. Jack turned out to be extremely intelligent and was quickly taught to help that handicapped tower opera-tor by pumping water and cleaning the ram-shackle cabin. Each morning Jack would push his master to work in a handcart. The hairy helper even learned to help run the switch tower, pushing and pulling the levers, setting the signals, and opening and closing switches on the siding. Jack was indeed a remarkable animal, and when he died in 1890, he left an amazing record. In his nine years as Wide's switch tower assistant, he never made a mis-take! And that's the way to run a railroad. Now, if we could only find another baboon to help run our government.

TIME ON YOUR HAND—OR WRIST

Time tells on a man—especially a good time. While that may be true, telling time in the good old days of the 18th century was something that influential gentlemen did with great flair. Back in those days if you were wealthy enough to own a watch, and educated enough to use it, you carried it on a dangling chain or fob, in a vest pocket. Men told time with a brief but impressive ritual, like taking the timepiece from the pocket, lifting the cover, looking wise, and then intoning the time as though revealing a great secret. The thing that put an end to this was the invention of the wristwatch. Who invented it, and why? Credit a Frenchman. His name was Louis Cartier, a well-known jeweler who got a request from an early aviator in 1907. The busy pilot wanted an easier way to check his flying time in speed trials without all the trouble of going to his pocket watch. And so, Messr. Cartier strapped a watch to a strap and then strapped it to the pilot's wrist, and voilà! The wristwatch was born. Its greatest popularity came during World War I when French soldiers found it extremely convenient. Needless to say, the wristwatch caught on. My wife has 150 of them.

A MASTER CHEF

It all began over 3,000 years ago when the Chinese made noodles from rice and bean flour. Those noodles delighted Marco Polo, and so when he returned to Italy from China around the end of the 13th century, he brought the noodle recipe with him. They called it pasta—a dough paste. The clever Italians made this paste into many forms—lasagna, vermicelli, ravioli, and spaghetti. I love 'em all. In the 1920s and 1930s, there was a chef named Hector Boiardi who worked at the posh Plaza Hotel in New York and felt that Americans weren't as familiar with Italian food as they should be, and decided to do something about it. He did. He bottled, canned, and sold his own spaghetti and ravioli. Folks seemed to like these convenient pasta dinners, and so did the great A&P grocery chain. They changed the spelling of Boiardi's name, put it on a colorful label, and faster'n you can say "spicy meataball," Boy-ar-dee's foods appeared on grocery store shelves across the United States, creating a minor culinary revolution, introducing millions of non–Italian Americans to their first taste of Italian cuisine, which probably led to the wonderful proliferation of authentic Italian restaurants—and "atsa good idée."

SOUR GRAPES

Everyday oft-used expressions come from every conceivable time, place, person, and thing. Here's a familiar one that comes from a fable. Ah, you ask. What's a fable? Well, by definition a fable is a story that makes a point. It's a short narration that enforces some useful truth—especially one in which animals speak and act like human beings. Anyway, back in ancient Greece there was a storyteller named Aesop who made good use of his fables. For instance, there's Aesop's fable about a foxy fox named Reynard, who one day stole into a secluded vineyard where many succulent bunches of grapes hung ripe and ready for eating. "Alas, and alack," wrote Aesop, the grapes were fastened on a tall, tall trellis, just a little too high for the sly fox to reach. And so, as pooped-out as he was, he just gave up, and cried out in frustration, "Take them who will! The grapes are sour!" And that's why today when you can't get something that's out of your reach, folks say your attitude is one of "sour grapes." And at today's prices, even grapes that are sour are expensive—as if you didn't know.

ONE FROM COLUMN "A"

If chop suey didn't come from China, then where did chop suey originate? And the answer is, in New York in 1896. Here's how. There was, at the time, a great Chinese statesman named Li-Hung-Chang who stopped off in New York while making a trip around the world. He invited many of his American friends to dinner in Chinatown, where many special Chinese foods are prepared. One of the dishes pleased one of the guests so much that she asked the chef just what the heck it was. The chef explained that it was chop suey, which in Chinese means a "mixture" or a kind of "hash." It was the chef's own creation. It wasn't long before the Chinese restaurant owners in the Big Apple, wanting to capitalize on Li's name and the well-publicized incident at his dinner, began serving various mixtures of meat, vegetables, and bean and bamboo sprouts under the names "Li-Hung-Chang Chop Suey" or "Li-Hung-Chang Rice," which were seasoned to suit the American patrons' taste. And of course, even now, there is no set way of making chop suey. The dish is *unknown* in China. The Chinese think it's too rich and some Americans think it's become too expensive. But everyone seems to love it. Me too!

BIG APPLE?

The English mathematician and natural philosopher Sir Isaac Newton, considered by many to be the greatest scientist who ever lived, did all of his important scientific work before he became England's master-of-the-mint in 1699. And while his scientific contributions are fundamental and famous, Sir Isaac's mother insisted that he drop out of school when he was a teenager. She hoped that he'd become a successful farmer. Sometimes a mother isn't always right. Isaac Newton gave the world such important discoveries as calculus—the branch of math that studies continuously changing quantities and is the basis for much of today's modern math. He also discovered the law of universal gravitation with most of the basic laws of mechanics. Amazingly, he was only 23 years old at the time of these discoveries. And the story of the apple? It's true. Newton described it himself. He said he saw an apple fall to the ground on a moonlit night and pondered whether the moon was held in the grip of the same force that the apple was. Of course, the rest is history. The part of the legend that isn't true, however, is that the apple hit Newton on the head.

INSIDE INFORMATION

It's been said that you should never argue with your doctor. He's got inside information, and some of that information is oftimes startling. For instance, to keep your feet warm, put on a hat, because 80 percent of all body heat escapes through your head. It's also interesting to note that most people by the age of 60 have lost 50 percent of their taste buds and 40 percent of their ability to smell. Maybe that's why senior citizens are often much easier to please when it comes to pretentious restaurants. And did you know that the heart beats faster during a brisk walk or heated argument than during sexual intercourse? And that the average adult human body contains 60,000 miles of vessels that carry blood to every part of the body, except the cornea. The cornea takes its oxygen directly from the air. And here's something hard to believe. Each square inch of human skin consists of 19,000,000 cells, 60 hairs, 90 oil glands, 19 feet of blood vessels, 625 sweat glands, and 19,000 sensory cells! One more strange fact. The daughters of a mother who's color-blind and a father with normal vision will have normal vision, but the sons will be color-blind! Some things are just not fair.

CHARLIE PARKHURST

We all know how difficult it is to keep a secret. Old-fashioned thinking had it that it was even more difficult for a woman to keep a secret. Well, maybe not. Take the case of old Charlie Parkhurst. In 1851 he signed on with the California Stage Company, hauling freight and passengers, and quickly became one of the most rugged, rough and tough stage drivers in the Wild West. He fought, he gambled, he drank, and once during a holdup, when the masked bandits ordered him to throw down his weapon and get off the stagecoach, Charlie Parkhurst promptly shot the leader of the gang and escaped with the strongbox and passengers intact. Another time, as a rickety bridge became even more unstable, brave Charlie raced his team across and reached the other side as the span collapsed. Charlie really looked the part—wore buckskins, was 5'8" with broad shoulders, and chewed tobacco. Ah, but sadly, as it must to all men, death came to Charlie Parkhurst on the last day of 1879, in a lonely cabin near Watsonville, California. When he was undressed and prepared for burial, his secret that he'd kept almost all his life was finally discovered. Tough old Charlie had really been a woman!

I'M OK, YOU'RE OK—OK?

Where the heck does the expression "OK" come from? Well sir, in 1840 Martin Van Buren ran for reelection as president and since he was a native of Kinderhook, New York, he was affectionately called "Old Kinderhook"—or O.K. for short. The campaign slogan became "OK with Old Kinderhook" and the cry resounded at political rallies everywhere. The letters were placed on placards and campaign signs. Even political cartoons of the day always carried some reference to the 15th and 11th letters of our alphabet. OK? Foreign coverage of the

presidential campaign was more than extensive. Europe and Latin America had an insatiable curiosity. They wanted to know not only who was running for office, but also who was running for cover. The humorous and biting cartoons became popular, and so did OK as an easy form of approval. So, since 1840, OK has become a part of almost every language on earth, the most widely accepted word form in history rivaled only by Coca-Cola, but that's another story. OK?

FLYING SORCERERS

Meteorologists are always studying the skies. The question is, do they report flying saucers when they see them? Well, sir, back in the days of the Arabian Nights astronomers reported seeing magicians on flying carpets, who, of course, were called flying sorcerers. However, the only meteorologist I ever met who believed in flying saucers was some smart aleck who pinched a waitress. Out of the thousands of meteorologists and astronomers who continually pay attention to atmospheric conditions, whose work depends on understanding visual phenomena, not one has ever verified in any way the existence of an extraterrestrial spaceship. The records show that 81 percent of saucer reports can be explained rationally, with the other 19 percent defying some kind of classification—about 50 percent of the time. It's that small percentage of unexplained sightings that lead people to believe that there's something out there that does not bear a "Made on Earth" label. What do you think?

DOUBLE TROUBLE

They say that all marriages are happy. It's just living together afterward that causes all the trouble. If that's true, then just consider the original Siamese twins, born in Siam in 1811. The brothers were joined at the chest by an armlike band of flesh and spent their entire lives no more than six inches apart. When they were 17 years old a Scottish merchant brought them to America where P. T. Barnum made the twins an almost instant show-biz success. The strange thing is that they not only hated P. T. Barnum, but hated each other as well. When they had earned enough money, they bought a farm in North Carolina and left show business. Then, wonder of wonders, they married two sisters, Sarah and Adelaide Yates, and proceeded to sire 21 children between them. As they aged, they fought even more and built two separate homes, spending three days in each. What they did on the seventh day isn't quite clear. Their names were Chang and Eng. Chang liked to drink; Eng liked to stay up late and play poker. And it's interesting to think about the problems they had when they had a disagreement. They lived into their sixties. Chang died of a liver ailment, and Eng, though healthy, died within hours of Chang's death since they both shared only one liver. And you think you've got troubles.

KEEP COOL WITH CAL

We know that James Madison, our fourth president, was only 5'4" tall and weighed 100 pounds. We know that the first president to ride on a railroad train was Andrew Jackson in 1833. But do we know whom historians consider the laziest chief executive in the nation's history? Of course we do. It was old Cal Coolidge, our 30th president. They say that he had a unique "genius for inactivity" because he averaged ten hours of sleep a day and ten hours of loafing, with barely four hours of work. His schedule rarely varied. Up at 6:00 AM, at his desk by 9:00 AM, lunch at 12:30 then a two-hour nap, and then back to his desk at 4:00 in the afternoon. He knocked off work by 6:00, and was in bed by 10:00. You'd think that with such a rigorous schedule Calvin Coolidge would need a vacation, and so each summer he'd head for the hills of South Dakota or northern New York where he'd hole up for three months. Often he'd disconnect the phone and run the country without a telephone. Well, apparently it worked in the 1920s. Do you suppose he'd get away with that today? I don't think so.

BIG AND BIGGER

Imagination is what sits up with a wife when her husband is out late. Imagination is what that great French writer, François Rabelais, used when he became tired of the extravagances and excesses of the French court of the 16th century. Rabelais wrote a wildly imaginative satire, an account of the life of an enormous king, a giant he named Gargantua. At birth, he wrote, Gargantua needed the milk of more than 17,000 cows. He rode to Paris on a horse as large as six elephants, and around the horse's neck he hung the bells of Notre Dame to jingle and jangle. Gargantua was so huge that he combed his hair with a comb 900 feet long, and it took 1,100 cowhides for the soles of his shoes alone. Of course, his appetite was prodigious, and he once made a salad from lettuce as large as walnut trees, and while doing that, he accidentally ate six travelers who'd hidden in the tree's limbs. We give you this interesting little Rabelaisian excerpt simply to show you how a word like Gargantua creeps into our language. If it's huge or gigantic—it's Gargantuan.

BIG BAD BOGIE

He was short, he was balding, and he spoke with a slight lisp—who? Why, one of the most popular actors of all time: the cult hero, the sad-eyed tough guy, Humphrey Bogart. Bogie's rough, tough screen image didn't match his real background. He was a gentle, almost shy man who came from a well-to-do New York family. He attended private schools and was slated to go to Yale and become a physician, like his father. But his poor school grades changed his career plans, and life upon the wicked stage called. He was an expert chess player, and while waiting for paying jobs he would earn rent money by hustling suckers in chess parlors on Sixth Avenue in New York. His appearances in the role of Duke Mantee in *The Petrified Forest,* on Broadway and in the movie, were turning points in his life. He appeared only once on television in 1955 as Duke Mantee with Lauren Bacall and Henry Fonda, for which he received $50,000—not bad for 1955—or even now. As for the lisp—no, it wasn't the result of a wartime injury. It was caused by a childhood accident in which a wound on his upper lip was stitched together by an inept doctor. Where the heck is a good lawyer when you need him?

SNAKES ALIVE!

You've seen pictures of this fascinating fact, read about it, and even seen it in Hollywood films to add mystery, danger, and intrigue to a story. The ancient and venerated tradition of snake charming in India is a showbiz practice that dates back to 300 BC. How do they charm snakes, anyhow? Not too difficult. All it takes is to be born into a family dedicated to the traditions of their forefathers and begin training around the age of five or six. Youngsters are taught snake handling by their fathers, who were taught by their fathers and so on back through the generations. The favorite snake to use is the cobra, famous for its dramatic arched posturing. Most folks think that the reptile is charmed by the reedy sound of the flute, but the truth is, snakes don't have ears; all snakes are stone deaf. The reason that the creepy-crawly snake-in-the-basket rears its unwholesome head is that the charmer lures him by use of physical gestures, such as swaying or rocking to and fro, or maybe just blowing a little cool air from the flute on the cobra's back to annoy it. The trick is to keep the snake interested, not angered, and not to annoy him so much that he strikes or slithers away. Some trick! And apparently that's all there is to snake charming. Just be sure you start your training at the age of five, and of course, pay no attention to the fact that many thousands of Indian natives die each year—from snakebite.

TICKING CRICKET—A NOISY THERMOMETER

We once heard of an Englishman who went to a cricket match and matched crickets. We've also heard that you can go out on a summer's night and listen to a cricket chirp the temperature. Is that true? Can a cricket really tell how warm it is? The answer is yes, but there's a catch—the temperature has to be between 45 and 80 degrees Fahrenheit before it'll work. If the temperature is above 80 degrees you'll get a cricket that'll chirp himself into a nervous breakdown because the higher the temperature the faster the cricket chirps. And when it gets too hot, it's good-bye Mr. Chirps! However, if the temperature falls into that 45–80 degree bracket, then the temperature is easy to figure out. Count the chirps for 15 seconds and add 37, and by Jiminy, that's how warm it is. 'Course it's a lot easier if you just turn on the radio and listen to the weatherman give you the information. And we all know weathermen are never wrong. Which is like saying free advice is worth the price.

MAUSOLUS'S TOMB

Once upon a time in Asia Minor in 400 BC, there was a small kingdom known as Caria. The king of Caria was a man named Mausolus. Old King Mausolus didn't do much that would make anyone remember him. He was pretty much a bust as a figure of history. The only thing in his favor was that his wife, who, in the peculiar customs of the time, was also his sister, simply adored him. Anyhow, when Mausolus died in 353 BC, his wife, Queen Artemisia, was inconsolable. She was so grief-stricken and depressed that, it was said, she had her husband's ashes collected, and each sad day she added a portion of them to her daily drink. Now, that's what I call devotion. Queen Artemisia gathered architects and sculptors and ordered them to erect a monument. And so a great marble building whose base measures 250 feet square with marble statues in prominence was planned and started. Back in those times this building was considered one of the Seven Wonders of the World. It was still standing at the time of the Crusades. The saddened queen died just two years after her great love, long before this monumental building was completed, and when this memorial was finished they called it Mausoleum, in honor of King Mausolus—which is why we call a sepulcher, a tomb, a burial vault, a mausoleum. Now you know.

IT'S ALL GREEK TO ME

There's a small, smiling, pot-bellied philosopher of Greek origin named Butsicaris who sits around with a pencil between his toes (for footnotes) who has the answer to most questions. So I asked him if he'd ever seen an eight-legged animal. "Okto," he replied, "means *eight,* and pous means *foot.*" The Greeks had a word for it, for indeed octopus means "eight-legged." Contrary to the terrifying reputation of this devilfish, the octopus is actually timid and retiring and deathly afraid of anything larger than he is. And while there are unconfirmed reports of sensational monsters, it is rare to find one larger than three feet across. There are over 100 varieties of octopi and some are so small that, full grown, they could fit into a thimble and still have enough room left over for 69 grains of salt and a TV critic's heart. For hundreds of years scientists thought that the "ink" an octopus squirted was merely a smoke screen so that enemies couldn't find him. But recent tests have shown that it actually disorients the ability of his sharp-toothed predators to find him by their sense of smell. The "ink" has no effect on human skin and does no harm to fishes swimming through it. Maybe it's also for old-fashioned fountain pens that still write under water—just thought you might like to know.

"K" IS FOR KODAK

Kodak means film and photography all over the world, but what does the word Kodak really mean? Is it a man's name? Is it an acronym? Well, it's actually just a name that George Eastman made up. Back in 1881 a fellow named David Houston invented a camera that used a continuous roll of film. He sold the patent to George Eastman for $5,700, and smart George promptly formed a photography company that's known throughout the world. But first he had to have the trademark—a word that was short, euphonious, and meaningless.

Since the letter K was his favorite letter he began experimenting with various combinations of letters, coming up with words that began and ended with "K." One of the words he coined struck his fancy; it was "Kodak." It seemed to fit the ideal trademark requirements. He didn't even have to take it into a darkroom and see what developed. He loved it, adopted it, and in 1888 registered it under the name Eastman Kodak Company of Rochester, New York. It's been in focus ever since.

THE TIN KING'S GOLD WEDDING

Simón Iturri Patiño was a businessman in Bolivia. He controlled over 50 percent of Bolivia's tin industry and became known as the "Bolivian Tin King." His personal fortune was estimated as being larger than his country's national budget and he was considered to be one of the five richest men in the world. This was noteworthy in itself, but his real claim to fame was the gift he gave his daughter as a dowry when she decided to marry a Spanish grandee in 1929. The regal reception was held in the grand salon of a magnificent mansion in Paris. All of Parisian society held its breath as the proud papa gave her a check, a check that was displayed in a glass case in the middle of that grand salon. Not only displayed, but highlighted by bright red and green spotlights to give it a more dramatic flair as the guests flowed and freeloaded at the grand reception. How big was that check? Bigger than most lottery prizes, and bigger than an elephant's earache. The check was for over $22 million—the largest dowry ever recorded! And just to add a little flavor, the father of the bride gave the newlyweds five Rolls Royces. And you thought a toaster and a hearty handclasp were enough.

MELBA WAS A PEACH

Back in the 1890s there was an opera star named Nellie Melba, who was adored by opera lovers around the world. And while she was a magnificent coloratura soprano and had a distinguished career, she's remembered today not because she was so great but because a chef at the Savoy Hotel in London worshiped her. The chef's name was Auguste Escoffier, a name that still crops up when discussing world-class cookery. Escoffier was so taken with Nellie Melba that he created a dessert that became the talk of the town. He loved Madame Melba so much in the role of Elsa, in Wagner's *Lohengrin,* that Escoffier's creation took the form of a swan, with great wings carved from blocks of ice, coated in iced sugar, and filled with vanilla ice cream, topped with peaches and raspberry sauce. He called it Peach Melba! Of course, you can still get this rich and imaginative dessert in fancy restaurants, without the block of ice, unless you insist. And while stout Nellie Melba loved the dessert, she had to watch her diet, so chef Escoffier devised something that she ate for breakfast every morning with her tea—Melba toast—a dry, brittle, crisp, toasted piece of bread so thin you could read through it.

MORSEL MANIA

It's been said that a man is showing his age when he looks at the food and not at the waitress. Sometimes the food is more attractive. Anyhow, food was certainly on the mind of Vincent Holt, an eccentric English author, in 1885 when he wrote a book titled *Why Not Eat Insects?* He felt that there was an unaccountable prejudice against eating insects and other unappetizing creatures. After all, he maintained, the consumption of insects was worldwide. Hottentots ate grasshoppers, ants are eaten in parts of southern Africa, worms are a delicacy in parts of Mexico, in Thailand large water bugs are gobbled with lip-smacking delight, and early Indians ate locusts. Holt's book not only documented the history of insect-eating people but included recipes for beetles, caterpillars, termites, and butterflies. He claims that bugs are rich in protein and make a pleasant change from the ordinary diet. Such a menu might not be mouth watering, but Holt maintains that insects are nutritionally sound eating. They go well with chicken, mutton, and fish. You'll have to decide for yourself, however, if you're adventurous enough to try a beetle on your burger. Remember, you are what you eat—and I like rump roast.

COCKY ROACHES

Way back in the dim dark past of creation, farther back than 350 million years ago, even before Madame Butterfly was a cocoon, there came into being one of the hardiest little creatures on earth. A scurrying, six-legged insect that was here when the Rockies were formed. His hardiness rivals that of Superman. We're talking about the lowly cockroach. He's actually a living fossil and has adapted better than any other living creature. He can be found anywhere on the globe. He can survive on paint, soap, beer, and gravy spots on ties, can eat his own cast-off skin, and can even digest wood. He can live a month without food or water, and five months on dry food without water. Actually, the cockroach is not as filthy as you might think; the thing that's misleading is his foul odor, a result of his scent glands—a means of protection from his predators. After all, who wants to eat a smelly bug? There are 3,500 species of cockroaches in a variety of sizes ranging from smaller than a grain of rice to as large as a hummingbird. They can even fly, but only as a last resort. And it's a pretty good bet that they'll be here long after we're gone, or, as we've often said, "Show me an arrogant insect, and I'll show you a cocky roach!"

HAM ON RYE, PLEASE!

Two slices of bread with meat, cheese, or some other food behind them is called a sandwich—as if you didn't know. How did the word *sandwich* originate? It comes from the name of the fourth Earl of Sandwich, who lived in the time of George III, the same nobleman after whom Captain James Cook named the Sandwich Islands, which later became the popular Hawaiian Islands. Anyhow, the sandwich was a great favorite with the earl. You see, he was a notorious gambler and often became so engrossed in his cards that he wouldn't stop to eat his meals. Instead, he'd have a servant put meat between two pieces of bread, which he ate without leaving the gaming table. While the earl gave his name to the sandwich, he really wasn't the first to eat bread and meat in that combination. The sandwich, under different names, was popular in many countries since ancient times. For instance, the Romans called a sandwich an *offula,* which means a bit or a morsel, and so the sandwich may well have been introduced in England by the Romans, nearly 1,800 years before the Earl of Sandwich was born. As for me, I'll take a peanut butter and jelly, please.

YOU ARE WHAT YOU EAT

Who said, "He was a brave man who first ate an oyster"? As far as can be determined it was first uttered and laughed at by none other than King James I of England. The sentence can be found in a book written by Thomas Fuller in 1662, and is recorded as, "He was a very valiant man that first adventured on eating oysters." No earlier reference to the saying has been found anywhere. In 1731 the brilliant satirist Jonathan Swift, in a book titled *Polite Conversation,* also used the phrase. Which proves that it was a proverbial saying even in the early 18th century. The first person ever to eat an oyster probably lived thousands of years ago, and it's not too likely that he was imbued with any particular valor or bravery. In all probability oysters were among the primitive and natural foods of mankind, being found along the seacoasts in many parts of the world. Oysters were first eaten because they were easy to find and because they're nourishing and wholesome when fresh or properly preserved. Ah, there's nothing moister than an oyster. Just make sure you have enough cocktail sauce to cover up the taste.

Some philosopher of long ago said, "There are only two great blessings in life—the love of art and the art of love." And for those of you who love art, consider one of the most notable paintings of the past 500 years: *The Last Supper* by Leonardo da Vinci—a true Renaissance man. Strangely enough, this painting as we know it today can in *no* way be considered an original. Here's why: Leonardo painted his masterpiece on the wall of a monastery in Milan between 1495 and 1497, but at the time it wasn't really appreciated. By 1517 the work was seriously damaged by dampness and was merely a mass of blots. In the 17th century monks who lived in the monastery seemingly had no respect for the work and broke a doorway through Christ's legs. The painting continued to decay, and in 1796 a garrison of French soldiers occupied the room, quartered their horses in the same room, and even used the wall for target practice. In World War II sandbags were piled against the painting to protect it from bombing. And wouldn't you know it—a bomb landed squarely on the monastery and destroyed everything—except the painting. Time and abuse just about destroyed this marvelous painting, and so *The Last Supper* you see today is a heavily restored work. Only outlines and a few brushstrokes are by the great da Vinci—but certainly, it's still worth seeing.

PLAY CRACK THE WHIP

Most of us know what a whip is, and most of us know what a legislative body is, so how did they get together and become a phrase that we hear from time to time? That is, "congressional whip." Just what the heck is a congressional whip? First the definition, then the origin. A whip, in a legislative body, is a member elected to the job of rounding up the members of his party and getting them to vote on bills in which the party has special interest. That's party politics. Now, why call the guy in the prestigious position a whip? Like so many things, we borrowed the term from the British Parliament, who borrowed it from, of all things, the fox hunt. You see, in hunting slang, the "whipper-in" or "whip" is the hunter's assistant who manages the dogs and keeps them from straying by driving them back into the pack with a whip. Now you can see how appropriate the term is as the "congressional whip" sort of "whips" the voters in the right direction and keeps them from straying. So far there've been no reports of whiplash injuries. And speaking of fox hunts, it was Oscar Wilde who said that "fox hunting is the pursuit of the inedible by the unspeakable."

PISH-TUSH AND POSH

There are certain words in the English language that conjure up images just by saying them out loud. Take, for instance, the word *posh*. It sounds like someone has just dunked a hot poker into a bucket of water. Posh! Actually, the word as we use it today means something swanky, deluxe, fashionable, and expensive. And where does a word like that come from? Well, there's an old wives' tale, a folktale, if you will, that the first letters of the phrase, Portside Out, Starboard Home, spells P.O.S.H. and refers to the ideal accommodations on a ship bound for India by way of the Suez Canal. Eastbound, the cabin's on the shady side, westbound, the cabin's on the sheltered side. The only trouble with this plan is that those ideal conditions vary with the seasons and don't necessarily work out that way. The truth of the matter is that the word *posh* can be traced back to the 17th century in England, when gypsies and small-time thieves used it simply as another word for *money*. The word was in use a long time before the passage was offered by the Peninsula and Eastern Steamship Lines, who, when questioned about the posh story said "they'd never heard of the acronym." And there goes another good story.

CENTER STAGE

If you want to get in the public eye without irritating it, the first thing you have to do is get into the "limelight." Where does the expression "limelight" come from you ask? Well, "limelight" was originally theatrical slang, and came about because a British army officer and surveyor named Thomas Drummond needed a better way to make distant surveying stations visible. He cleverly took an oxyhydrogen flame, directed it onto a cylinder of lime, and produced a steady, intense, white light that could be seen as far as 60 miles away. He called it the "Drummond Light" and not only used it as a surveying aid but also adapted it for use in lighthouses. In 1825, long before the use of electricity, there was really no adequate way of lighting the stage in theaters, and so Drummond's light was quickly adapted for theatrical use. Lime-lit stage lights, floodlights, and spotlights soon became commonplace. Of course, the limelight was equipped with a lens so that it could be concentrated on a particular point on the stage where the most important action was taking place. In the process of time, the leading player in the piece was said to be "in the limelight." Glad we could throw a little light on the subject.

LOST IN TRANSLATION

To a scientist, not knowing can be mighty frustrating. But at least in one case, for over 300 years ignorance can be the fount of knowledge. Have you ever wondered how that funny-looking animal with a pocket in its pants, the kangaroo, got its name? According to legend, the explorer Captain James Cook and the noted naturalist Sir Joseph Banks, while exploring the eastern coast of Australia in 1770, left their ship, the *Endeavour,* and discovered a strange, bouncing, six-foot-tall animal that could leap 20–30 feet in a single bound. Of course, these trained observers asked the natives what they called these interesting animals. The natives replied, "Kangaroo." Captain Cook and Sir Joseph Banks duly noted this in their log. Well, for the next 50 years or more, explorers and naturalists were unable to find any tribe in Australia that used the word *kangaroo* in reference to an animal. What they did find, though, was that the natives that Cook and Banks had talked to were indeed saying "kangaroo" which, in their dialect, meant "I don't know!" And that's how the kangaroo accidentally got its name. Ah, yes, the kangaroo— a jumpy animal because it's usually left holding the bag, and so are the etymologists as they try to pin down the origination of the word.

BOX IT OR BAG IT!

If you've ever been in England or Canada around Christmastime you've probably heard of Boxing Day. Just what the heck is Boxing Day and does it have anything to do with pugilism? Nope, nothing at all to do with the prize ring. It all stems from medieval times when the monks of certain orders used to offer Mass for the safety of ships and at the same time place a small box on each ship to receive contributions from the sailors. The idea of a box for contributions carried over into placing containers or boxes in churches around Christmastime for donations to be distributed to the poor. This custom, over time, developed into what is now called Boxing Day. It's observed the day *after* Christmas, and on this day the Christmas boxes, hopefully filled with casual contributions, are opened and given to those who render small services. Which is why on the 26th of December, in England and Canada, small appreciative gifts are given to mailmen, delivery boys, doormen, newsboys, and so on—a day late, but, well, better late than never. Ain't that the truth?

OH!... I WAS EXPECTING A LETHAL SOUTHERN CONCOCTION OF RUM AND ORANGE JUICE THAT CUSTOMARILY IS SERVED IN A BIG SILVER BOWL WITH A MESS OF EIGHT-FOOT STRAWS

A LITTLE ZING IN HIS STING

Can a scorpion kill you? And will a scorpion commit suicide by stinging himself to death if you pour a ring of gasoline around him and set the ring on fire? Both beliefs are as phony as a marble toupee. As for scorpions, if you've seen one, you've seen them all, in a manner of speaking, because all 400 kinds of scorpions are basically alike. These creepy little eight-legged creatures range in size from one to eight inches in length. Their abdomen ends in a sort of segmented tail that curves gracefully over the back and waves in all directions—like an actress arriving at a cocktail party. At the end of this tail is a stinger loaded with enough poison to knock off the insects he eats. You might say he has a little zing in his sting. But what if he stings you—is it lights out and make out your will? Nope—although he has enough poison to cause a pretty painful wound and scare you half to death, it's not enough to really harm a human, at least there's no record of one having killed a full-grown man. But then, they don't seem to keep records of half-grown men. The scorpion eats nothing but insects and hunts mostly at night. Nonetheless, if you find a scorpion, be careful and leave him alone—even if you were born under the sign of Scorpio.

LITTLE ARMORED THING

Way back when a Spanish adventurer named Cortez and his pantalooned plunderers came to the New World to see what they could see, they not only copped a peek at the Pacific but discovered a quick, quaint, queer little creature that seemed to be wearing a coat of armor, much the same as they did. So they called this animal the armadillo or "little armored thing." He's not much of a fighter—lover, yes, but fighter, no. He can't even bite because his teeth are way back in his mouth, none in the front. But eating poses no problem since he dines on ants, termites, mice, eggs, or an occasional tasty snake. For protection he simply curls up into a tight ball and hopes his thick hide discourages his enemies from biting. But the fox or dog, who like armadillos for lunch, aren't dummies. They simply roll the armadillo over and get at his not-so-protected abdomen, or roll him into a pool of water where he has to unroll to get a breath of air—which is, alas, usually his last. All armadillos look pretty much the same—a ladies' purse with legs, or a miniature tank with a live head. About the only thing they don't do is clank!

DOG TURNING

Nearly everyone has seen a dog turn around several times before lying down. Even old Charles Darwin said he'd seen a dog turn around 20 times before settling down in a comfortable position. Why do dogs do that? According to behavioral scientists, dogs do this because of plain, old-fashioned heredity. Since domestic dogs are descended from wild dogs or wolves, and since these animals lived in the forest or brush, they had to trample down the grass or vegetation in order to find a suitable place to rest. This ancient bed-making process still survives as an instinct in the domestic dog. It's inborn, and like any longtime habit, it's hard to break. And so, when Rover or Prince or King or Sweet Patootie is tired and sleepy, his ancestors' habit is revived, and whether on a rug or in a rec room, he turns around and tramples the imaginary vegetation into a comfortable bed for the night—unless he's a very wealthy dog who owns his own profitable "barking lot." And then I suppose he has someone else do it for him.

BLIND PIG

Work, say the comics, is the curse of the drinking class! Well, whatever you think of alcohol and its use and abuse, don't you sometimes wonder where the expression "blind pig" comes from? Of course, a blind pig is an unlicensed saloon or after-hours joint that sells liquor illegally. During the 1920s and 1930s, in the time of Prohibition, "blind pigs" were sometimes called "speakeasies," because you had to speak easy and use a password to get into the illegal club. Anyhow, the phrase "blind pig" goes back to 1838 when the state of Massachusetts passed a statute limiting the sale of hard liquor. It didn't take long for the more enterprising citizens to find a way around that law. They set up little shops or booths and advertised that a marvelous striped pig could be seen inside for a small fee. A fee, strangely enough, that was equivalent of the price of a glass of booze. When the customer went inside he really found a pig with stripes. A clay pig with painted-on stripes, and standing nearby was a glass of whiskey. The term "blind" in this case meant something hidden or secret, which proves that there's more than one way to skin a cat. But whichever way you do it, the cat won't be too happy.

ADVERTISING WILL GIVE YOU A HADDOCK

Advertising, they say, is the art of making people think they've always wanted something they've never heard of before—the effective power of words. For instance, fishermen many years ago used to catch fish that were very tasty. Canneries put them up in attractive cans and labeled them exactly what they were, "horse mackerel." Not many people, however, bought the product. Who wants to eat horse mackerel? So, the wise ones who did the advertising changed the name to tuna fish. Well, the mackerel sold much better under that name. But then there was resistance to the pallid color of the fish—too pale, too white—and sales still weren't high enough. So, back to semantics and back to the advertising agency. The answer was simple. They put the words "top-grade tuna—guaranteed not to turn pink in the can" on the label. Of course, that was no lie, and in nothing flat the buying public accepted the product. Success at last! The trademark, Chicken of the Sea, hasn't hurt sales either. And as a facetious ad man once said after he heard the story of Samson and Delilah, "Samson had the right idea about advertising—he took two columns and brought down the house."

DRACULA'S BLOOD RELATIVE

Think of something that makes your skin crawl, your heart pound, your blood race, your hair stand on end, and is as dangerous as standing at the wrong end of a shooting gallery. No—not the IRS! We're talking about a flying mammal called the vampire bat, a gruesome little horror that gave Bram Stoker the idea for his chilling book *Dracula*. Vampire bats don't actually suck blood, but they do lap it up greedily. If they find a sleeping animal they'll land nearby and scuttle toward it like some huge hairy spider. They have two scalpel-like front teeth with which they scoop a trough in the skin and then move about so the head rests at the bottom of this wound, and when the trickle begins, so does dinner. The victim is rarely awakened. These unsavory creatures live in caves, hollow trees, old houses, and just about any other place they can find to hang their heads. They range from Argentina to the southern United States in countless millions and could be a serious threat since they transmit a great number of diseases with their bite. The vampire bat has one real claim to fame though. He's the only mammal that's a true parasite. Why didn't Noah knock them both off when he had the chance?

WHAT A NUT

Did you know that the Queen of Sheba was a pistachio nut? She loved 'em. Pistachios originated in the Middle East, growing wild in the deserts in ancient times. They were a rare delicacy and so expensive that only royalty could afford them—and they're not cheap even now. But why are some pistachios dyed red and some left that soft ivory color?

As you might suspect it had to do with money. You see, when they were first put into vending machines pistachios had to be a little more appealing and attractive than the pale cashews and peanuts that were also sold from vending machines. So pistachios were dyed bright red with harmless vegetable dye; this all started—the dyeing that is—in about 1930. Aside from making pistachios more attractive, another reason for the red color was the fact that from the time they're harvested until the time they're shipped the glossy tan hull gets stained and blotched and the aesthetic appeal is equivalent to soup stains on neckties. Folks might think they're spoiled—which, of course, they aren't. Besides, I like red fingernails. They make your fingers look so healthy.

BAKER'S DOZEN, OR UNLUCKY "13"

Back in the 15th century in merry old England, butchers, bakers, and candlestick makers weren't considered the most honest of tradesmen—especially the bakers. It seems that bakers in those days had a habit of shortchanging the customers by using a big thumb on the scales when they weighed the goods. And so laws were passed to deal with this little scam. Well, the bakers became wary, and so, just to make sure that they gave their customers all they had coming, the bakers put an extra muffin or cake in the package. That is, making sure that their 12 muffins really weighed what they were supposed to weigh. They wanted to stay on the safe side of the new law, which is how 12 became 13. In other words, that's how a baker's dozen came about. But what about the superstition surrounding the number 13? Where did that come from? The answer is from the Last Supper. You see, Jesus and his 12 disciples sat down at the Last Supper and within a day Christ had been crucified and Judas hanged himself. And so it came to pass that people believed that whenever 13 persons sat down to dine together, at least one would die within a year. From that the superstition spread. I'll knock on wood.

Henry Ford, the original, was a close friend of Thomas Alva Edison, both members of the mutual admiration society. Both geniuses in their own right. Ford so admired Edison that he had Edison's Menlo Park laboratory and workshop moved stick by stick, board by board, tool by tool, item by item to Greenfield Village and reassembled. Included in the move was the lab where the incandescent light was actually invented. Ford went so far as to have the dirt around the building dug up and placed around the building's new location, including the original pieces of discarded glass, nails, and refuse. Greenfield Village is a collection of historic buildings next to the Henry Ford Museum in Dearborn, Michigan. It is said that when Edison lay dying in 1931, Ford asked Edison's son, Charles, to hold a test tube next to his father's mouth to catch his last breath. You see, old Henry believed in reincarnation and thought the spirit left the body with one's last breath and therefore wanted to collect the essence of Edison. Of course, some say he just wanted a souvenir. In any event, when Henry Ford died in 1950, the test tube was discovered among his personal belongings, still tightly sealed and apparently still containing the last breath of the great inventor. If you get a chance to visit the fine Henry Ford Museum, you can see this test tube with its mysterious contents—it's on display there. Wouldn't you just love to pull the cork and hear the great man's last sigh? Well, maybe.

YOU'RE FIRED!

It's been said that you should never raise your hand to a child, because it leaves your midsection unprotected. And never tell your boss exactly what you think of him. You may be left holding the bag or getting the sack. Just where did the expression "getting the sack" come from? And why does it mean being fired or discharged? It all started way before the Industrial Revolution when most artisans and mechanics lived on the job. If they ever moved or got a new job, they of course gathered their belongings, put the tools of their trade in a sack, and hit the road for greener pastures. When they got to their new job, their belongings went into their living quarters but the sack of tools was left with their employers for safekeeping. Now if the artisan or mechanic was no longer needed, if business was bad, or if he told the boss what he thought of him, the poor guy, who had no protective union, was promptly discharged. And to make sure the employee didn't misunderstand, the employer gave him back his sack of tools. He literally "got the sack." I hate when that happens. Then, as my wife says, the most popular labor-saving device today is still a husband with money.

SWEET SAINT SWITHIN

Ever heard of St. Swithin's Day? Why it's the day we celebrate every July 15. Way back in the ninth century there was a Bishop of Winchester who was much loved and, more important, a performer of miracles. His last wish, just before he died in 862, was that he be buried in the churchyard where the "sweet rain of heaven" would fall upon his last resting place. One hundred years later the church declared Bishop Swithin a saint and they decided a saint should be entombed *inside* the cathedral proper. July 15 was set aside as the day Bishop Swithin's body would be dug up and then reburied *inside* with all the pomp and circumstance a saint should get.

They paid no attention to Saint Swithin's final wish about being buried in the churchyard, and so another miracle was wrought. On July 15 it began to rain—not just a dust settler but a real gully-washer, and it continued to rain for 40 days, which, of course, put an end to the reburial plans. Ever since then, so says the legend, if it rains on St. Swithin's Day it'll continue to rain for 40 days. If it's a fair day, it'll be fair for 40 days. And that's how legends are born. Or as we often say, let a smile be your umbrella—if you like to gargle rain.

PRELUDE TO DISASTER

There are those who maintain that how you die is just as important as how you live. Well, you might get an argument there. Anyhow, consider the vanity of Archduke Francis Ferdinand of Austria. Whenever he had to attend an occasion of great magnitude, he had himself sewn into his uniform so that there wouldn't be a single crease to mar his appearance. Well, he was wearing one of his sewn-on uniforms on June 28, 1914, when an assassin leapt from the crowd and shot the well-dressed duke. It was impossible to unbutton his uniform, and by the time scissors were found, the archduke had bled to death. Then there was an imaginative tailor in France named Tiechelt, who in 1911 devised a bat-wing cape that he firmly believed would enable him to fly. Incredibly, he got permission from the police to test his exciting invention from the Eiffel Tower. And so, at eight o'clock on a cold December morning, friends, reporters, and photographers watched apprehensively as M. Tiechelt climbed over the rail on the Eiffel Tower, spread his cloth wings, and plunged to his death! Sometimes the last thing a man wants to do is the last thing he does.

TAXIDERMIST'S DELIGHT

Once upon a time there was a cowboy who was so bowlegged that they hung him over the door for good luck. It wasn't Roy Rogers, whose real name was Leonard Sly, because Roy wasn't bowlegged. Successful and wealthy, yes, but bowlegged, no. The popular singing cowboy had a horse named Trigger, a taxidermist's delight. Trigger is stuffed, as they say, and so is his dog, Bullet, and wife Dale's mare, Buttermilk. It all may seem a little barbaric, but once you've seen them all tastefully displayed in the interesting Roy Rogers Museum in Apple Valley, California, I think you might have a different perspective. It all came about when young Roy visited the Will Rogers Ranch, which had been turned into a western museum, and found it almost barren. He made up his mind then that if he ever made it big in show business, he'd save everything—and he did. But of all the things that he treasured, Trigger was at the head of the list. After all, you can't always find a horse that was house-broken, could count to 25 by stamping his hoof, and could even sign an "X" in a hotel register with a pen gripped in his teeth. Rather than bury Trigger, he had him stuffed, which makes a lot of sense to a lot of animal lovers. As for Roy and Dale, well, wax museums are good enough for humans.

LEAD FOOT, DEAD FOOT

James Dean, the rebellious youth, the anti-establishment hero of the young in the 1950s, the legend who refused to die, got his first professional acting job in the early 1950s riding a merry-go-round in a Coca-Cola commercial. He was picked for the commercial because he looked like a typical all-American boy. He was good-looking alright, but did you know he didn't have any front teeth and had to wear a special bridge to cover the gap? Occasionally, to shock people, he would flash a smile without the bridge, which gave him a menacing, vampirish look. Obviously he had a good sense of humor.

His starring role in *East of Eden* established him as a rising star. He was really on his way. Then in late 1955 he filmed a TV spot about driving safety. In that spot he said, "Sure, racing is dangerous, but I'd rather take my chances on the track any day than on the highway. Drive safely, because the life you save may be *mine*." A few weeks later, James Dean died in a car crash while driving his Porsche to a racing competition in Salinas, California. Ironically, just two hours before the accident he was given a ticket for speeding. What a loss.

GREYFRIARS BOBBY

In the city of Edinburgh, Scotland, back in the mid-1800s, a burly policeman named Jock Gray adopted a little Skye Terrier, a stray dog that became so attached to his master that he never left his side. Most mornings they would stop at a café for breakfast. For years the dog and that policeman were inseparable, then the policeman unfortunately died. Three days after his death, the perky little terrier showed up at the café as usual. The owners tossed him something to eat, as usual. But the faithful pup carried his meal to his master's grave before he would eat a mouthful. The dog's name was Bobby, to be exact, and for the next 14 years he showed up every morning at the café, picked up his lunch, and returned to the gravesite *before* he ate. Aside from that, he never left his master's grave—not even for a moment. All of Edinburgh grew to know and love this loyal little pooch and saw to it that he always had food and shelter. Bobby kept his loving vigil until he died in 1872, and was buried, of course, near his master's grave. There's even a statue of Greyfriars Bobby in Edinburgh—the little stray whose loyalty made him famous.

GETTING RID OF YOUR OVERHEAD

Way back in the mid-1750s in France, there lived a doctor, a relatively compassionate man, Dr. Joseph Ignace Guillotine. He was a sensitive and intelligent doctor who was a member of the National Assembly during the French Revolution. Violence, mayhem, social change, and just plain bloodletting were the order of the revolution. Hanging dissidents was as commonplace as rice in a Chinese restaurant. And so, in a much publicized speech to the assembly in 1789, the good doctor argued for a neater, quicker, and more humane way to kill commoners. Hanging was too painful and drawn out, he argued. He urged the use of a new beheading device he'd heard about, and because of that speech, the French began calling the head chopper a guillotine—a word that lives on, even though Dr. Guillotine neither invented the killing machine nor died by it. He actually died in 1814 from an infected carbuncle on his shoulder. You might say that the guillotine was a real pain in the neck for Louis XVI. You might say it was the first real cure for dandruff. You might say that—but I won't.

A FEW FUN FACTS

Most folks like to collect little bits of information that, most times, are as important as a quart of water going over Niagara Falls. But they're fun facts, liven the conversation, and bring smiles or arguments whenever they're used. For instance, did you know that there are 293 ways to make change for a dollar? That at 90 degrees below zero Fahrenheit your breath will freeze in midair and fall to the ground? And here's something interesting you might try at your next party, just to see if the research is correct. When asked to name a color, three out of five people will say "red." And did you know that the dog featured in the box of Cracker Jacks was named Bingo, and that the little sailor boy's name was Jack? And did you know that the reason Wall Street in New York is named Wall Street is because in 1654 residents built a wooden blockade, or wall, across a small section of lower Manhattan? Why'd they build it? Simply to protect themselves against a possible attack by Indians. And for those of you who think today's justice is too lenient, consider the strange fact that in 1740 a cow was found guilty of sorcery in France and publicly hanged. Ah, yes, fun-filled facts and nuggets of knowledge, indeed.

CHINCHILLAS CHOOSE CHILE

Have you ever wondered what makes caviar so expensive? Well sir, you have to consider that it's a full year's work for the sturgeon. And what makes chinchilla so expensive? Well sir, it takes the lives of over 100 of the tiny animals to make just one coat. The poor little creatures are only about ten inches long, and obviously some of them aren't going to measure up. So the furrier has to really match and mate before he comes up with a garment that can rival the late Liberace's dinner jacket. The chinchilla looks something like a wealthy squirrel, with a sort of rabbitlike head, but the fur— ah, the fur—has the softness of down, the delicacy of gossamer, the fullness of Raquel Welch, and the exquisite color of a pale, blue-gray sky at dusk. One single strand cannot be seen by the naked eye, which means that it's finer than a stingy spider's silken web. About the only place in the world that the chinchilla lives in the wild is Chile, high in the mountains. In 1923 the little animals were close to extinction, but 18 worried little chinchillas were brought into the United States and the beginning of the chinchilla farm was born. The danger has passed. Nine years is the average life span of a chinchilla—if nobody needs a coat.

UNDER THE INFLUENCE

Once upon a time in a mythical city, there was the apocryphal story of the town drunk who fell down two flights of stairs while carrying two fifths of bourbon and didn't spill a drop. He kept his mouth closed! While in jolly old England, there's a true story that's almost as bizarre. A section of London, a parish called St. Giles, became the scene of one of the strangest floods in history. On October 17, 1814, a nearby brewery, its giant brewing vats filled with enough beer to flood a city or at least part of one, had one of its giant vats burst. Within moments, 3,500 barrels of beer rushed and roared wildly into the parish of St. Giles, a slumlike region where entire families were crowded into one-room flats, and the really poor lived in wretched conditions in basements. The river of beer slammed into buildings, swept victims off their feet, and buried them in debris. Rescuers had to wade in alcoholic suds up to their waists. And when the strange flood finally subsided, nine people were dead and three houses totally destroyed. Alcohol can cause big trouble in more ways than one, I guess.

DON'T CRY FOR ME, ARGENTINA

"Don't Cry for Me, Argentina," a very popular song from the musical *Evita,* refers to the beautiful wife of Juan Perón, then president of that South American country. Eva Perón died in 1952 at the young age of 33, and her politically powerful husband ordered her embalmed immediately and to lie in state. What makes the story unique is that the doctor who embalmed her took a full year to do the job— using a special preservation that seemingly would last forever. Now the story becomes bizarre. President Perón was ousted before Evita would be buried, and so she was placed in a warehouse, where she promptly got lost in the packing case shuffle. Soldiers found the coffin a couple of years later and shipped it to the Argentinean embassy in West Germany and it was stored in the basement there. Someone then sent it to Rome. They didn't want it, so they sent her to Milan and there she stayed until 1971 when Juan Perón, in exile in Spain, found out where she was and had the casket sent to Madrid. He pried it open, and wonder of wonders, in 19 years Evita looked just as beautiful in death as in life! And here's the most bizarre twist of all—Perón and his third wife, Isabel, used to dine nightly in the company of the casket of Evita. Talk about strange dinner companions!

Contributors

Sonny Eliot
Humorist and Weatherman

Sonny Eliot's career began at WWJ-TV, now WDIV, in 1946. Rumor has it that Eliot's was the first face ever to appear on Detroit TV . . . not true, says Sonny, but it's a good legend.

Much like the man who came to dinner, he was called to do a bit part on a local variety show produced by WWJ-TV and ended up staying 35 years. While there he hosted a variety of programs including the 17-year series *At the Zoo*, and Hudson's perennial Thanksgiving Day Parade. Eliot also appeared on children's programs, quiz shows, comedy-variety stanzas, specials, commercials, and a multitude of other program classifications, but he earned his greatest reputation as a television weathercaster. For several years he also hosted a television movie and is currently heard on WWJ Newsradio 950 with his unique weather presentation that premiered on WWJ-AM in 1950.

Sonny's been making Detroiters smile about the weather for years. Unlike any other in the

171

country, Eliot's weathercasts are a mixture of fast-paced humor, bits of far-out philosophy, one liners, improbable analogies and similes, and, not to be overlooked, easy-to-understand weather forecasts. The National Association of TV Program Executives (NATPE) has named his witty reports the nation's best.

Born and raised in Detroit, Michigan, Sonny attended high school in Detroit and received a B.A. degree in English and an M.A. in mass communication from Wayne State University, where he began his broadcasting and acting. He has appeared on network radio shows such as *The Lone Ranger, The Green Hornet,* and *Challenge of the Yukon.* On stage, he appeared at Will-O-Way Playhouse, the Sun Parlor Playhouse in Leamington, Ontario, opposite George C. Scott, and Detroit's Northland Playhouse and Vanguard Theatre.

During World War II, Eliot was a B-24 bomber pilot; he was shot down over Germany and spent the next 18 months as a prisoner of war in Stalag-luft I. While in captivity he lifted the morale of the other prisoners by staging original skits and revues. He holds the rank of lieutenant colonel in the U.S. Air Force Reserve and was named Air Force Liaison Officer for the First Congressional District. His bomber group was awarded the Presidential Unit Citation and Sonny was also awarded the Distinguished Flying Cross, Air Medal, and Purple Heart.

Some of the many awards and citations Eliot received include the Sloan Award and citations by the American Legion, the American Meteorological Society, and the Toastmaster International Award. The Michigan Association of Broadcasters has awarded him the Broadcast Excellence Award in the Broadcast Personality or Team Category for Best of Category.

His book *Eliot's Ark* (1972) is a delightful collection of fact and fiction on animals, both friends and foes of man.

Caricature by George Fisher

**Draper Hill
Caricaturist**

Draper Hill is one of the most respected carica-
turists and political cartoonists today. He is also
a recognized scholar on the history of English
graphic satire, known in particular for his research
and writing on 19th-century English-language political cartoonists James Gillray, Thomas Nast, and
Joseph Keppler.

Draper graduated magna cum laude from
Harvard in 1957 where, as a freshman, his drawings began to appear on the cover of the *Harvard
Lampoon.* Later he served as the magazine's art
editor. He majored in American history and found
his calling at the intersection of politics, art, and
commentary.

He was the editorial cartoonist for the *Detroit
News* (1976–2000), cartoonist for the *Commercial Appeal,* Memphis, Tennessee (1971–76), the
Worcester Telegram, Worcester, Massachusetts
(1964–71); cartoonist, reporter, and illustrator
for the *Patriot Ledger,* Quincy, Massachusetts
(1957–60); and a regular contributor to *Preservation News,* Washington, D.C. (1968–81).

From 1960 to 1963 Draper attended the Slade School of Fine Arts, University College, London, under a Fulbright Grant.

Draper's work has been exhibited throughout the country, featured in exclusive exhibit catalogs, reprinted in major papers and national news magazines, and distributed by King Features Syndicate. His articles and columns have appeared in multiple publications including *Dial* magazine and the book review section of the *New York Times* as well as in the *Detroit News*. He also authored "Cartoons and Caricatures for Time-Life Books Encyclopedia of Collectibles" (1977).

Draper's books include *The Crane Library* (1962); *Mr. Gillray the Caricaturist* (1965); *Fashion-able Contrasts* (1966); *The Decline and Fall of the Gibbon* (with James Roper, 1974); *Introduction to Hugh Haynie: Perspective, Louisville* (1974); *"I Feel I Should Warn You . . ."* (1975); and *The Satirical Etchings of James Gillray* (1976).

"Cartooning is," as Hill writes, "an unstable compound of art and literature, of permanence and transience, of the creative and the parasitic . . . and art which depends on the perishable mix of conviction, nuance, suggestions and assault"; the political cartoonist "may discharge simultaneously the functions of moralist, entertainer, propagandist, and, inadvertently, historian."

Photo by Jim Morphew

Stanley D. Williams
Editor

Stan Williams grew up and still lives in the Detroit metropolitan area, where as a child he watched Sonny on television. Yes, watching the TV weather reports in Detroit with Sonny Eliot was pure entertainment. Stan also remembers clearly Sonny's live narration of *Tubby the Tuba* and *Festival of the Animals* at the Detroit Symphony's Saturday morning Young People's Concerts that his mother dragged him to.

Stan holds a Ph.D. in communications–film studies (1998, Wayne State University); an M.A. in speech-communications (1980, Eastern Michigan University); and a B.A. in physics (1969, Greenville College, Greenville, IL).

Today, Stan is an international award-winning video producer, filmmaker, author, and live show creator with hundreds of projects to his credit. He has also written, edited, and managed hundreds of publications and documents for Fortune 100 companies, as well as his own enterprise. After college, Stan spent several years as an electronic engineer training astronauts for NASA's first space station, Skylab.

175

He is the author of the Hollywood screenplay structure book *The Moral Premise: Harnessing Virtue and Vice for Box Office Success* (2006), the executive producer of SWC Films, which is involved in the development and production of various film and television products, and the owner of Nineveh's Crossing, a digital media distribution company.

Sources

Breland, Osmond P. 1948. *Animal Facts and Fallacies*. New York: Harper and Brothers.

Burnah, Tom. 1986. *The Dictionary of Mis-Information*. New York: Harper and Row.

Ciardi, John. 1987. *Good Words to You*. New York: Harper and Row.

Feldman, David. 1987. *Why Do Clocks Run Clockwise?* New York: Harper-Collins.

———. 1989. *When Do Fish Sleep?* New York: Harper Perennial.

———. 1990. *Why Do Dogs Have Wet Noses?* New York: Harper-Collins.

Hardy, Elizabeth, ed. 1978. *One Thousand Questions & Answers*. Lynx Press.

Louis, David. 1983. *2201 Fascinating Facts*. New York: Ridge Press.

Panati, Charles. 1987. *Panati's Extraordinary Origins*. New York: Harper and Row.

Shenkhan, Richard. 1991. *I Love Paul Revere, Whether He Rode or Not*. New York: Harper-Collins.

Stimpson, George. 1946. *A Book about a Thousand Things*. New York: Harper and Brothers.

Sutton, Caroline. 1981. *How Do They Do That?* New York: Morrow Hilton Press.

Tuleja, Tad. 1987. *Curious Customs: The Stories behind 296 Popular American Rituals*. New York: Harper and Brothers.

CD Track Listing

The audio CD that accompanies this book includes 26 stories read by Sonny Eliot, as well as a bonus interview with cartoonist Draper Hill. Page numbers correspond to the locations of the stories within this volume.

BONUS TRACKS
An Interview with Draper Hill

Recording Engineers: Tom Force, WWJ; Stan Williams, SWC Films
CD Mastering: Stan Williams, SWC Films